40
UNSTOPPABLE
WOMEN

Who Changed the World

Harold J. Sala

AspirePress

40 Unstoppable Women Who Changed the World
Copyright © 2021 Harold J. Sala
Published by Aspire Press
An imprint of Hendrickson Publishing Group
Rose Publishing, LLC
P.O. Box 3473
Peabody, Massachusetts 01961-3473 USA
www.HendricksonPublishingGroup.com

ISBN 978-1-6286-2965-1

All Scripture quotations, unless otherwise indicated, are taken from the Holy Bible, New International Version®, NIV®. Copyright ©1973, 1978, 1984, 2011 by Biblica, Inc.™ Used by permission of Zondervan. All rights reserved worldwide. www.zondervan.com The "niv" and "New International Version" are trademarks registered in the United States Patent and Trademark Office by Biblica, Inc.™

Scripture quotations marked (ESV) are taken from The ESV® Bible (The Holy Bible, English Standard Version®), copyright © 2001 by Crossway, a publishing ministry of Good News Publishers. Used by permission. All rights reserved.

Scripture quotations marked (MSG) are taken from THE MESSAGE, copyright © 1993, 2002, 2018 by Eugene H. Peterson. Used by permission of NavPress. All rights reserved. Represented by Tyndale House Publishers, a Division of Tyndale House Ministries.

Scripture quotations marked (NKJV) taken from the New King James Version®. Copyright © 1982 by Thomas Nelson. Used by permission. All rights reserved.

Scripture quotations marked (NLT) are taken from the Holy Bible, New Living Translation, copyright ©1996, 2004, 2015 by Tyndale House Foundation. Used by permission of Tyndale House Publishers, a Division of Tyndale House Ministries, Carol Stream, Illinois 60188. All rights reserved.

Scripture quotations marked (CEB) are taken from the COMMON ENGLISH BIBLE. © Copyright 2011 COMMON ENGLISH BIBLE. All rights reserved. Used by permission. (www.CommonEnglishBible.com).

The statements and opinions expressed in this book are solely those of the author and do not necessarily reflect the views of Rose Publishing, LLC or that of its affiliates. Citation of a work does not mean endorsement of all its contents or of other works by the same author(s).

Book design by Cristalle Kishi.

Photo of Joni Eareckson Tada used with permission by Joni and Friends International Disability Center; Photo of Mother Teresa by John Matthew Smith.

Printed in the United States of America
010121VP

All of us need inspiration. Dr. Harold Sala's *40 Unstoppable Women* will give it to you! I hope that learning about these remarkable women whets the appetite of many others to want to know how God forms people like these. Each story is brief so that busy women with little time to read can be inspired, too. You will finish each one wishing there was more to read!

GAIL MACDONALD
Author, *In His Everlasting Arms*

I personally know the power of real-life stories to inspire and change a life, and I am delighted that Dr. Sala has collected these short vignettes of powerful women—some well-known and some who are seemingly obscure. A life well-lived has lessons to teach the next generation.

KAREN KEEGAN
President, M&K Ministry
Co-author, *Diamond Fractal*

For the past fifty-five years or so, Dr. Harold Sala has been busy teaching, preaching, broadcasting, and writing about Jesus. And along the way, he has authored more than sixty books that have been published in some nineteen languages. *40 Unstoppable Women* may prove to be his most practical book yet. Whether this book is read in a classroom or a living room, it is destined to stir the hearts of its readers as it lays out some well-worn paths to follow.

SHERRY WOREL
Founder, Stoneybrooke Christian School

Within the pages of *40 Unstoppable Women* are many hidden secrets of women that turned into incredible examples of courage and strength. The examples of these incredibly faithful women will help you see new ways that you can reflect God's power in your own life! And may they encourage you to make a difference in your world as well.

GEORGALYN WILKINSON, PHD
President, Gospel Literature International

From ordinary to extraordinary, these featured women chose (and those who are still with us are still choosing) the way of the cross over the life of comfort, convenience, and compromise. The brilliance of Dr. Sala shines through as he invites readers to see themselves in each of these women.

MARY KAY PARK, PHD
Global Media Professional, Speaker,
and Adjunct Professor of Intercultural Studies

In this book, Dr. Harold Sala succinctly gives us inspiring examples of women who stepped out in faith, made great sacrifices, and allowed their lives to shine—giving hope to a dark and lost world. I highly recommend this book, most especially to women who desire to make a difference through the immeasurable riches of His grace and power. As you read this inspiring book, may it give birth to a desire in your heart to be used by God for his glory.

MARIE CAPARROS
Administrator, International Bible Institute of Cebu

[These] are women of substance, women of grit. Strong and competent, they defy the stereotype that virtuous women are better seen not heard. In the face of suffering and life's challenges, or taking on huge responsibilities, these God-loving women from different continents and generations have inspired and will continue to inspire us with their compelling stories of exceptional courage and fierce determination. Kudos to Dr. Harold Sala, again, for clinching another great read. And thanks for your appreciation of women of strength and character.

GRACE SHANGKUAN KOO, PHD
Professor of Educational Psychology, University of the Philippines
Author, *Guarding Your Heart and Mind* and *Work Worth Doing Well*

A transformative book every woman should read! The personal stories will pierce the hearts of everyone with takeaway questions that will challenge readers to change for the better or realize that one can do the impossible! Dr. Sala has given a different perspective on how and what people can do to make a difference in this generation.

MARJORIE S. VILLANUEVA
President and Managing Director, Design Amoire, Inc.

40 Unstoppable Women [is] a mosaic of many lives—one big picture illustrating many unique stories—all of which are very motivational. As I read them, God spoke to my heart, asking, "Are you ready to do impossible things for me?"

YANA KRYUCHKOVA
Educator and Translator

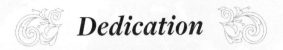

Dedication

I would indeed be remiss if I failed to dedicate this book to the two wonderful women who have impacted my life as have no others.

The first would be my mother, Ruby Edith, who lived out the virtues that I have written about.

The second would be Darlene, the woman who became my wife on December 23, 1959, and has been God's great gift to me—encouraging me, walking alongside me, sharing all the experiences God has sent our way.

Without their influence, not only would I not be the person that I am, but this book would never have been written! I will forever be grateful to God for them both.

Contents

Preface 11

1. Joni Eareckson Tada 13

2. Mommy Olga 17

3. Henrietta Mears 21

4. Sister Freda 25

5. Corrie ten Boom 29

6. Darlene Deibler Rose 33

7. Susanna Wesley 37

8. Florence Allshorn 41

9. Gladys Aylward 45

10. Michelle Ruetschle 49

11. Virginia Prodan 53

12. Mother Teresa 59

13. Gertrude Chambers 63

14. Mary Slessor 67

15. Lillian Trasher 71

16. Auntie Wang 75

17. Evangeline Booth 79

18. Trudy Kim 83

19. Florence Lin 87

20. Dr. Kim Pascual 91

21. Miriam Neff 97

22. Gracia Burnham 101

23. Elisabeth Elliot 105

24. Amy Carmichael 109

25. Maren Neilson 113

26. Svea Flood 117

27. Margaret Brand 121

28. Kim Phuc Phan Thi 125

29. Sheila Leech 129

30. Grace Agar 133

31. Mavis Orton 137

32. Nadia Pachenko 141

33. Edith Schaeffer 145

34. Rosa Parks 149

35. Jacquie Chevalier 153

36. Noah's Wife 157

37. Marjaana Seilonen 161

38. Helen Cadd 165

39. Graciela Lacey 169

40. Mary, the Mother of Jesus 173

Discovering the Path for Your Life 177

Preface

My granddaughter, Taylor, is just about to launch her career in medicine. She's a beautiful, strong, and gifted young woman who has grown up in a world that, by and large, has not held her back. She longs to be a world-changer.

It has been my privilege over the course of sixty-plus years in ministry to meet more than a few world-changers—remarkable men and women with incredible life stories. There is nothing better than the true story of how an individual has overcome what life has thrown at him or her, risen to enrich the lives of others, and changed the world. That's why I read at least one biography a week!

This collection of biographical sketches had to be written because many of the world-changers whose stories I share are unknown. I wanted to write of these women, many of whom I've known personally, because I knew their lives would inspire and encourage others.

But Taylor, and perhaps you too, may not know of the forty women whose stories are contained in this book. These are women who have gone before, as people of faith, grit, character, and courage. These are not women who were stopped by difficulty, disability, discrimination, or evil, but they are women who lived out their relationships with a personal, powerful God, no matter the cost. They answered the call of God upon their lives, blazing their own trails in their own unique adventures of faith. You will see that they were *unstoppable!*

You, too, are called by God to an unstoppable life. My prayer is that as you read about the lives of these forty incredible women, you will sense God's world-changing call upon your own life, the path he has for you. He is calling for more unstoppable women to change the world! I hope that this book helps you (and Taylor) answer the call.

Acknowledgments

I would like to extend my appreciation to Beng Alba Jones who edited my manuscript and gave me valuable insights to make this more readable. Beng is not only a great editor but has become a warm and personal friend. Thank you, Beng!

1

JONI EARECKSON TADA

The Unstoppable Woman

S he is a bestselling author, with her first book selling more than four million copies. She received over ten honorary degrees and has been the featured guest on countless high-profile television programs. She is a two-time breast cancer survivor who founded an organization that has provided wheelchairs to tens of thousands of people, and she served on the National Council on Disability which produced the Americans with Disabilities Act (ADA). With a tender and compassionate heart and an unforgettable message, she is a powerful voice for the disabled around the world.

Who is she and what is her story?

Her name is Joni Eareckson Tada, a woman with quadriplegia who is impacting our world. However, she hasn't always used a wheelchair. It was on a warm July day that seventeen-year-old Joni's life was forever changed after she dove into the too-shallow waters of the Chesapeake Bay. She was transported to a local hospital, and as a nurse strapped her to a gurney, Joni tried to move her arms and legs to no avail. "Can't you tell me what's happened to me?" she begged as nurses simply walked away. Following surgery, Joni found herself sandwiched inside a Stryker Frame that had to be rotated 180 degrees periodically. She lost movement and feeling in her body from her neck down.

Joni began to adjust to a routine that felt mechanical, including being attended to by caregivers who had no compassion and simply considered her to be waste of their time, awaiting her demise by a lack of willpower and the torture of suffering. Although she had become a believer in Jesus Christ through a Young Life ministry, she was still trying to find her own way and, by her own admission, "didn't have time for God." She fought against discouragement, wondering where God was in relation to her injury, and even despaired of life itself.

Friends, including boyfriends, faded away and left her with an emptiness that only the Lord could fill. "Before my accident, I didn't 'need' Christ," she wrote in her book *Joni*. "Now I needed him desperately."

Eventually, Joni was flown to California where a rehabilitation facility gave her excellent care. She learned to cope with her disability. In fact, she even learned how to clutch a pencil or a pen with her teeth and draw, amazing people with her artwork. Later on, she was able to propel an electric cart that gave her some mobility.

Well-meaning but off-the-wall individuals complicated her life. On one occasion, she was accosted in a parking lot by an overzealous young man. When he asked her if he could pray for her, she told him she never refused a prayer for healing. Then he launched into a memorized diatribe suggesting that if she would only confess her sin and have faith to believe, she would be healed and delivered once and for all.

But there was another man, Ken Tada, who came into her life and truly cared for her. This retired high school teacher became her husband and has been by her side since 1982—a wonderful companion and helpmeet for her.

For over forty years, the international organization she founded, Joni & Friends, has been bringing both practical resources and the hope of the gospel to countless people with disabilities. The latest chapter in Joni's life is that she has become a disability-rights activist who speaks on the issue with authority and understanding. Her book *When Is it Right to Die?* makes it clear that this right should be God's sovereign decision, affirming the position that so-called "mercy killings" are no less than taking a person's life.

Joni can look back on her years and all that she experienced and say with confidence, "God's hands stay on the wheel of your life from start to finish so that everything follows his intention for your life. This means your trials have more meaning—much more—than you realize."[1]

---

[1] Joni Eareckson Tada, *Pain and Providence* (Rose Publishing, 2012) 12.

Takeaway Thought

Are you limiting yourself and what you can do because of a disability, weakness, or deep insecurity? Plan to conquer a fear or take steps to do something great. The God who is giving Joni strength every day is the same God who can work in and through you today.

MORE ABOUT HER STORY

Joni: An Unforgettable Story by Joni Eareckson Tada (Zondervan, 1976, 2001)

2

MOMMY OLGA

The Woman Loved by Hundreds of Prisoners

Soon after my wife and I moved to the Philippines in 1974, I was invited to speak in one of the world's largest maximum-security prisons, known as Bilibid Prison, just outside Manila. I was met by Olga Robertson, a woman of Lebanese heritage with dark hair and piercing eyes. To the 9,000 inmates who were interred at that time, she was known as "Mommy Olga." Never will I forget seeing twenty-five prisoners who sang in the choir that morning as they formed a line before the service. Mommy Olga took a bottle of men's cologne and gently slapped some of it on both cheeks of men who were rapists, murderers, thieves, con artists, and outcasts of society. She, however, didn't see them as criminals but as her boys whom she loved, men who had been transformed by the gospel of Jesus Christ, who had received God's forgiveness regardless of what their futures held.

Following the service, she took us on a tour of the facility. A small cell on death row contained bunk beds for four men, an empty milk can used as a urinal, and swarms of flies and mosquitoes. The execution chamber was a tiny room that contained a wooden chair with multiple leather straps attached to restrain the victim, whose face would be covered with a leather mask.

Olga became a mother figure to hundreds of men who asked her to accompany them to their deaths, bringing comfort and the assurance that they, saved through the blood of Jesus, were about to enter heaven's portals. Men who were to be executed sang gospel songs and quoted Scripture as they were strapped to the electric chair, unafraid of what lay ahead.

What led her to this unique ministry? Following her marriage to an American serviceman, Olga had twin girls. When her American husband was shipped to the US, he broke off communication with Olga and their daughters. Learning to support herself following the occupation of the Japanese in World War II was next to impossible. Seeing that a Foursquare Church had been established near her work, Olga began attending and was soon converted. Eventually, Evelyn Thompson, a missionary, urged her to follow up on thirty prisoners who had received Christ but had no spiritual support. Olga agreed even at a great cost. She had to ride two buses, a jeepney, and a horse-drawn carriage in the sweltering heat to make it to Bilibid Prison. The following week Olga returned, taking a small choir with her. This time over a hundred men gathered to hear from her.

Did her presence make any difference? The prison superintendent can tell you. He began to notice the changes in the lives of the prisoners. Leaders of the fifteen different gangs in the prison stopped their hostilities toward others. Enemies became friends. When there were occasional prison riots, the superintendent would send in Olga to quell the riots. Because of her influence, a chapel was built, as well as a small house so Olga could be nearby. Money was contributed that allowed Olga to purchase an owner-type jeep (a kind of jeep with no doors) and prisoners taught her how to drive.

Did everything run smoothly? Not always. In fact, one time, angry prisoners took three hostages and forced Olga to drive the escape vehicle. When they reached the main gate, Olga slammed on the brakes and jumped out of the vehicle. Guards immediately executed the kidnappers.

But this traumatic experience didn't stop Olga from doing what God called her to do. Her heart overflowed with unquenchable love. When Olga was sixty years old, a prisoner told her that his wife was pregnant, and that if the child was a boy, he and his wife wanted Olga to adopt the child. Olga legally adopted the baby and named him Shalom. He grew up to love Jesus and followed in her footsteps in serving God.

Mommy Olga was a dedicated servant of the Lord whose love for prisoners was strong enough that she was willing to walk with these men to the death chamber as 220 volts of electricity took their lives. What great love!

Takeaway Thought

Are you ready to do the impossible and love the unlovable? Is prejudice keeping you from reaching people who need God? If Mommy Olga could learn to love prisoners, you, too, can open your heart to love others.

3

HENRIETTA MEARS

Public Energy Number One

She was an educator who founded Gospel Light Publishing, one of the twentieth century's leading Christian publishers. She was the force behind the National Sunday School Association in the US and the author of *What the Bible Is All About*, one of the most helpful books ever written about understanding the Bible. She established the Forest Home Christian Conference Center in Southern California, where, under her ministry, thousands of men and women have found purpose for their lives. It was here that Billy Graham became convinced that the Bible is the Word of God. (In fact, at the conference center stands a tree with a plaque commemorating the place where he made the decision never to doubt the Bible again.)

To understand what kind of person Dr. Henrietta Mears was, you must know that she was part of a culture and an era when World War II had ended, men and women had returned to somewhat of a normal life, and the Hollywood scene was exciting. I shall never forget meeting her for the first time. Arriving at the historic

Presbyterian Church of Hollywood, I found her office and entered. Dr. Mears's secretary led me into her room, where I was seated on a well-worn brown sofa to wait for her arrival. Suddenly, she swept into the room, and I stood to my feet. Without making small talk, she briskly said, "Sit down, young man. In the next two hours you will learn more about Christian education than you did all the time you were in school!"

She was known for her outrageous, eye-catching hats, generous nature, and no-nonsense approach to impacting the world. To get attention, she had her car painted green and yellow. She often said, "Small ideas do not inflame the minds of people," and that mentality—based on her conviction that she was serving a big God—was contagious. She was 100 percent committed to honoring and serving the Lord Jesus Christ and she expected her disciples to sign on to doing their best to save the world as she was. When faced with a nearly impossible situation, her response would be, "Let's pray about this right now!" She also believed that in addition to praying, God expected that those who prayed would move forward in faith, organizing both people and resources, and trusting that "God's work done God's way will never lack God's supply," something first articulated by Hudson Taylor, a nineteenth century missionary to China.

Dr. Lindquist, the pastor of the church where movie stars, wealthy men and women, and an army of ordinary people worshiped, called her "Public Energy Number One." Billy Graham wrote of her, "I doubt if any other woman outside of my wife and mother has had such a marked influence. Her gracious spirit, her devotional life, her steadfastness for the simple gospel, and her knowledge of the Bible have been a continual inspiration and amazement to me."[2]

If some individuals are born with a divinely-programmed calling, she is included in that group. Henrietta was the seventh child of a banker who at one time owned twenty banks. In kindergarten, she became bored and explained that it was designed "to amuse little children," adding, "and I'm amused enough. I want to be educated." At age seven, she decided that she wanted to be a Christian and joined a Baptist church. At the age of twenty, she contracted muscular rheumatism and doctors told her that if she continued her studies she would be blind by age thirty. She responded, "Then blind I shall be—but I want something in my head to think about."[3]

Traveling to California, where she thought that perhaps her health would be better, she visited the First Presbyterian Church of Hollywood. The pastor, who previously had spoken in the church where she grew up,

[2] Ethel May Baldwin and David Benson, *Henrietta Mears and How She Did It* (Regal Books, 1974), Preface.
[3] *Wikipedia.org*, s.v. "Henrietta Mears" (accessed March 9, 2018).

immediately offered her a position as Director of Christian Education. Henrietta said yes and she served in this capacity for the rest of her working years. In her heart was the conviction that every person is capable of going deeper and doing more for God than he or she is currently doing, something she demonstrated by her own life.

While Southern California was her home for many years, her influence went around the world. The Sunday school resources she helped develop were translated into numerous languages. Henrietta Mears is a powerful example of a woman who allowed God to use her passion and determination.

Takeaway Thought

How committed are you to learning something new about God, the Bible, and everything else that would contribute to your spiritual growth? Break out of spiritual complacency and be as passionate in your quest for knowledge and truth as Henrietta Mears.

MORE ABOUT HER STORY

Teacher: The Henrietta Mears Story by Marcus Brotherton (Tyndale House, 2016)

4

SISTER FREDA

The Woman Who Could Not Turn Away the Suffering

Freda Nyanga Mukhweso came into this world with a compassionate heart. The youngest of four children, she was born in Kenya in a mud hut with a thatched roof. As a young child, it was her responsibility to go to the river. For forty minutes, she would walk over rough, dusty ground scattered with small stones, leaving her feet bruised and bleeding. Who would ever have thought that a person with her background would later become the driving force behind one of the top nursing schools in Kenya. To date, she has touched the lives of thousands of hurting people. But what else do we know about her?

Freda's parents were poor tenant farmers who did their best to provide for the family, but there were never enough resources to alleviate their hunger and needs.

Even as a young person, Freda often reached out to those who had nothing, especially those who were sick and needy and had hopelessness in their eyes. From older women, she learned how to practice folk medicine and use local plants for treatment. For instance, she learned that when a mother giving birth begins to hemorrhage, chewing on pumpkin root would help stop the bleeding.

When she was a teenager, her life took a dramatic turn. After returning home from school, her parents informed her that they had chosen an older man she had never met for her to marry. Thus, at the age of fifteen, she was forced to marry because the "bride price" would allow her brothers to get an education. Friends, feeling sorry for her, smuggled books to her. She devoured these books. Three days after giving birth to her fourth child, she took the high school equivalency exam and passed it with flying colors. Shortly after that her marriage disintegrated.

In 1979, Freda was employed at Kenya's Mount Elgon Hospital. The administration, seeing both her ability and compassion for the sick, arranged for her to spend some time in Canada studying trends and issues in nursing, tropical diseases, and surgery. Thereafter, she was known as Sister Freda, since all nurses in Kenya are known as sisters.

Upon her return to Mount Elgon Hospital, there was a stirring in her heart when she saw the state of the district hospital. It was overcrowded. Sometimes three or even four patients would be confined in the same bed. When patients had no money, they were turned away. On her way to work, she would observe patients who were crawling on their hands and knees to the district hospital. Going home in the evening, she would see their cold, lifeless bodies lying by the side of the road. She was convinced that there should be a way to provide care for the poor. But how? God answered her question in the most unusual way.

Sister Freda provided nursing care for the wife of an Englishman, Richard Robinson, who had been born in Zambia but moved to Kenya. When Mrs. Robinson passed away, Richard was drawn to Sister Freda by her gracious demeanor and love for people. He began assisting her and provided the funds for a small two-room clinic where medical care was provided for those who were suffering, regardless of their ability to pay. After a six-year courtship and multiple proposals, Sister Freda and Richard were married.

Eventually, with the help of a group from Saddleback Church in the US, a small eight-bed clinic was constructed, and then a surgical center, followed by a feeding program for children, and later on, a nursing school, Nzoia College of Nursing, which today ranks as the number one school of nursing in Kenya.

What's the force that drives Sister Freda? It's prayer! Every morning she spends the first two hours of her day kneeling at a couple of well-worn hassocks. When asked, "How did you learn about prayer?" she replied, "I really learned about prayer for myself when as a child I was taking the milk to the market. Before I took the shortcut through the forest, I would stop and earnestly pray that

God would keep me safe from the wild animals, for the danger was very real. And he did just that!"[4]

Takeaway Thought

Is there a need that you can meet today? Do you know anybody who is suffering in body, soul, or spirit? The God who gave Sister Freda a heart of compassion might be prompting you to care for another person today. May your hands and feet be quick to move as you obey.

---

[4] Author interview (July 2007).

5

CORRIE TEN BOOM

The Saint Who Survived Ravensbrück

Should you have the opportunity to visit Amsterdam, take the train from Central Station for a twenty-minute ride to Haarlem, a delightful Dutch town. Walk past the city square and just off this point, past the old church where Corrie's nephew, Peter, was the organist, you will find a watch shop (now a museum) made famous by the book and movie *The Hiding Place*. In this place once lived the ten Booms, a family of committed Christians.

When World War II broke out, the ten Booms responded to the genocide of the Jewish people by making their home a safe house for Jews. This Dutch family would hide Jews and give them new identity papers, clothes, and money to escape the Gestapo's grasp.

But how did the Jews know when to come? Hanging in the window of the ten Boom's home was a small triangular sign advertising the famous Tissot watches made in Switzerland. When the sign was out, it was safe for Jews to enter, but when it was missing, this was a signal that they should come back at a later time. A neighbor,

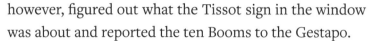

however, figured out what the Tissot sign in the window was about and reported the ten Booms to the Gestapo.

The entire ten Boom family was arrested, along with the people hiding in their home. Within a few days of captivity, Corrie's aged father died, and she and her sister Betsie were sent to Ravensbrück Concentration Camp, a women's labor camp in Germany. At the camp, Corrie and Betsie were lights in a dark place, initiating worship services and comforting the distressed and afflicted. But Betsie's health began to deteriorate. Still, she encouraged her sister Corrie, saying, "There is no pit so deep that he [God] is not deeper still."

Betsie died, and a week before Corrie's scheduled execution, through an administrative fluke, she was released while the other women in her age bracket were sent to the gas chambers. God had miraculously spared her life. After the devastating war ended, Corrie went back to Germany as an ambassador of goodwill, and wherever she went, she stressed the importance of forgiveness. But had she truly forgiven those who hurt her?

One evening, her message of reconciliation was put to the test. Having just spoken in a bombed-out church, she was standing in the front greeting people when she recognized a man walking down the aisle. It was one of the Ravensbrück guards who had been both cruel and crude to the women when they had first arrived at the camp. He was wearing an old brown topcoat and carried a hat in his hand. In Corrie's mind's eye, however, she saw the skull and crossbones on the visored cap of the SS guard and the altogether too familiar blue-gray soldier's uniform.

When he reached the front of the church, he extended his hand towards hers, saying what a fine message she had brought. Corrie was frozen. Hatred welled up in her heart. Touching him was the last thing she wanted to do, but she remembered how she had just told the people that if we do not forgive each other, God will not forgive us either.

"God," she prayed, "help me to forgive him." Corrie says a warm feeling began at the top of her head and surged through her body. She extended her hand and said, "I forgive you. ... I forgive you with all my heart."

Writing of that experience, she says, "Forgiveness is not an emotion. Forgiveness is an act of the will, and the will can function regardless of the temperature of the heart."[5]

After the war, Corrie traveled the world. She often told the remarkable story of the hiding place in their little home at Haarlem where scores of people found refuge and shelter. The hiding place is where God gave her family the courage to help change the world.

---

[5] Corrie ten Boom and Jamie Buckingham, *Tramp for the Lord* (CLC Publications, 1974), 81–85.

Takeaway Thought

Imagine how incredibly hard it must have been for Corrie ten Boom to extend forgiveness to her former tormentor. But she did it through the grace of God. Are you finding it difficult to forgive a particular person? Trust God to soften your heart. You need to be set free from the prison of hatred and bitterness today.

MORE ABOUT HER STORY

The Hiding Place by Corrie ten Boom
(Chosen Books, 1971)

6

DARLENE DEIBLER ROSE

A Woman of Incredible Hope and Strength

To compress the story of a woman whose life experiences are as compelling as Darlene Deibler Rose's into the space of several hundred words is challenging and nearly impossible. Such, however, is the impact of her story. In 1938, along with her husband Russell, Darlene landed on Batavia, Java (known as Jakarta today) on their first wedding anniversary. They were privileged to serve as missionaries in New Guinea, where Darlene was the first Caucasian woman ever to be introduced to the tribal groups. The tribal people were fascinated with Darlene's white skin, so different from theirs.

Then Pearl Harbor was bombed by the Japanese and it became apparent that the Japanese intended to take New Guinea as well. Darlene and Russell were advised to leave on a Dutch ship that was evacuating foreigners. Their missionary field chairman urged them to leave immediately. However, after praying earnestly, both Darlene and Russell felt that God wanted them to remain where they were ministering. This decision proved fortuitous, as the Dutch ship was torpedoed and sank with no survivors.

The Japanese systematically began to take control. All the men were seized, and as Russell was taken prisoner, he said, "Remember one thing, dear; God said that he would never leave us nor forsake us." She never saw him again. Shortly thereafter, she was taken to a prisoner of war camp where the camp commander, Mr. Yamaji, was notoriously vicious and cruel.

In *Evidence Not Seen*, a book she wrote so that her two sons would know what their mother had endured, she tells the amazing story of her survival. Dysentery, hunger, blood-sucking mosquitoes, and sadistic guards made her life almost unbearable. Interrogations, beatings, and putrid-smelling food began to gnaw away at her health. While she was accused of being an American plant (her citizenship was actually Dutch), the women in her barracks knew her as a believer in Jesus Christ.

Darlene became acquainted with Mr. Yamaji when the women in her barracks selected her to represent them. In a perverse sort of way, he expressed his respect for her when he called her to his office to give his condolences on her husband's death. She responded by telling him that she did not hate him, saying that God had placed her there by his will, and explaining the plan of salvation to him. Years later, she heard from another person that Mr. Yamaji had repented of his sins and had become a believer in Jesus Christ as a result of Darlene's input.

Prisoners were tortured and some, striving to please their captors, accused each other (including Darlene) of being spies and liars. Loving these accusers was difficult, yet she did everything in her power to alleviate their suffering and help others. On one occasion, she was placed in a cell on death row. Darlene was suffering from dysentery, malaria, and beriberi all at the same time, but God supernaturally healed her of all three afflictions.

Four long years slowly passed. Then the tide of the battle changed and, to the great relief and joy of those in the concentration camp, American bombers began strafing the prison. However, this move also filled the hearts of the women with fear that they might die at the hands of American bombers instead of the cruelty of the Japanese. Then, as the war was about to end (though the prisoners were unaware of this), Darlene was forced to write a false confession of activity against the Japanese and the executioner's sword was drawn. But before she could be killed, Javan government officials arrived and she was saved from the executioner's grasp.

American bombers then began to drop relief packages, and Darlene was called in and told by authorities that the war was over. For someone who had lived with the shadow of death hanging over her head for so long, freedom was challenging. US personnel arranged for her to return to a changed country. She had no idea how to contact her parents, how to book a flight on an airplane, or how to find money to purchase clothes and basic necessities. God, however, provided for her needs.

Her rehabilitation and recovery, both emotional and physical, was a slow process. She eventually remarried and returned to New Guinea as a missionary. Her courage and commitment in the midst of terrifying experiences came from her unflinching faith in God and her determination to show his love even to her enemies.

Takeaway Thought

When you are stripped of everything, how far do you think you can go? Darlene Deibler Rose, whose freedom was taken away from her, managed to survive in captivity. Whatever is taking you captive right now—whether in body, soul, or spirit—take comfort in the fact that we have a God who sets captives free.

MORE ABOUT HER STORY

Evidence Not Seen: A Woman's Miraculous Faith in the Jungles of World War II by Darlene Deibler Rose (HarperOne, 1990)

7

SUSANNA WESLEY

*A Woman with Convictions of Steel
and a Heart of Love*

When my wife and I visited London, where I ministered as a young preacher, one of our first excursions was to take the tram to Bunhill Fields, a cemetery where some of the most radical figures of history are buried. Founded in the 1660s as a burial ground for nonconformists and dissenters, it held the remains of at least 120,000 people including famous individuals such as John Bunyan, author of *Pilgrim's Progress*; Daniel Defoe, writer of *Robinson Crusoe*; the poet William Blake; and a woman of destiny: Susanna Wesley, the mother of John and Charles Wesley.

Who was Susanna Wesley and how did she impact our world? She was born in 1669, the twenty-fifth child (yes, twenty-fifth!) of a strong-willed Puritan father, a man of renown in his own right. Without question, Susanna inherited her father's convictions and strong will. Her mother was a woman with strength of character and the ability to run a household of an unusually large family.

Susanna absorbed both her strength of character and her organizational ability, something that was eventually passed on to her sons, John and Charles, founders of the Methodist Church.

Eric Metaxas writes in his book *7 Women and the Secret of Their Greatness*, "It can be said without exaggeration that John and Charles Wesley's efforts—their evangelism and service to the poor, the disenfranchised, and the hopeless—changed the world. It also can be said without exaggeration that who these great men were and all they did in their lives had everything to do with the extraordinary woman who raised them."

Susanna was thirteen when she met nineteen-year-old Samuel Wesley at a social event. Six years later, they were married. From the beginning, theirs was not what would be considered a "good marriage" today. Once, when Susanna adamantly refused to say "Amen" when her husband prayed for a king whom Susanna thought to be an inadequate leader, her husband abandoned her and the children for six months. Another difficulty that haunted her for her entire life was that her husband was constantly in debt and could never adequately provide for them. A third cross she had to bear was her subjection to an insecure husband who felt threatened by his wife's strong opinions and abilities.

When Susanna believed their local church was not providing enough instruction for her children, she began gathering the children in the kitchen each Sunday afternoon and teaching them herself. Soon friends and neighbors joined them, and she read a printed sermon of her pastor husband's, in spite of his objection to the leadership of his wife.

Her challenges didn't stop there. Twice her home was burned to the ground. She faced criticism for doing what she was convinced was right, but she endured. After her children left home, she wrote long letters of instruction and warned them of worldly sins they would encounter.

There are no limits to what God can do through anybody who has convictions and is willing to pour her life out in leading, training, and discipling the next generation. Such was the case when Susanna Wesley came into the world.

Takeaway Thought

Do you have people around you who could use a mentor? If not children, maybe you have young relatives or friends who can benefit from somebody who can love, guide, and train them to righteousness. Susanna Wesley sacrificially took the time to teach and shape her children and the world changed because of it.

MORE ABOUT HER STORY

7 Women and the Secret of Their Greatness
by Eric Metaxas (Thomas Nelson, 2015)

8

FLORENCE ALLSHORN

The Woman Who Refused to Quit

Near the end of the nineteenth century in Britain, when Florence Allshorn was three, her father, a doctor, died. She and her two brothers were brought up by a governess described as "a kind but undemonstrative lady of strict background." Eventually, her brothers were sent to a boarding school, and Florence's courage brought her through the difficult days of childhood.

In her teen years, she came under the influence of Dr. Gresford-Jones, who later became the bishop of Uganda. During those years, Florence fell in love with Jesus and developed a servant's heart. She wrote to a friend, "I'm not content with goodness and niceness and duty, which I've struggled for. Now I want Him."

This passion for Christ led Florence to serve as a missionary in Uganda under the Church Missionary Society. While there, she quickly discovered why everyone who had preceded her called it quits. The problem wasn't the cockroaches, or the plague, or even the headhunters who preyed in the bush. The number one problem was the senior missionary, a woman who would get so upset that she would go without even speaking to Florence for days at a time. Other women had attempted to serve with this missionary but gave up and went home. Florence herself almost quit. After all, she had every reason to pack up and head home.

What did she do to cope with the cold shoulder treatment she received? She read 1 Corinthians 13 every day and prayed for the senior missionary. You are expecting that prayer changed the heart of this senior missionary, right? I don't know for sure. But I do know that prayer changed Florence and the way she looked at her colleague. In her diary, she wrote these touching words: "To love an individual means to accept him as he is. If you wait to love him till he has gotten rid of his faults, you are loving an idea. Love him as he is with the painful expectancy that he can be different. Only then are we loving with the love of Christ."

The lessons that Florence learned through difficult times served as the impetus for her future ministry. After four very taxing years in Uganda, health issues forced Florence to return to England. She thought that after rest and recuperation she would be able to go back to Uganda. But when the doctors discovered a cavity in one of her lungs, the diagnosis felt like a death sentence. She had lost both her mother and brother to tuberculosis. Florence refused surgery, even if it meant living with only one functioning lung. She wrote, "Faith is not an easy thing to come by. You are fortunate if you have been ill enough to think that only faith will save you. Then you have to have it, when your body is saying the opposite. You can gull yourself about the soul, not the body. To believe that God is stronger than the enemy and He has looked on you, His creation, and said, 'It is very good.'"

After she spent a year in Switzerland to regain some of her strength, the Church Missionary Society invited her to temporarily take over their two small training colleges for women. This led to an innovative phase of missionary preparation with emphasis on relationships with fellow missionaries. Out of this came the establishment of a facility known as St. Julian's, where communal living taught the hard lessons that would be needed on the mission field. A co-laborer observed, "Florence had the ability, often lacking in strong personalities, to inspire rather than control." Her goal in life was to help people find "the peace that lies on the other side of the conflict" and "the healing alchemy of love." How desperately do we need this today!

Takeaway Thought

There is no guarantee that you will get along with everyone you meet. Have you ever given up on people because they were like porcupines—that is, they prick and hurt you whenever they're near? Follow the example of Florence Allshorn and look for ways to live in harmony with others no matter how difficult the circumstances might be.

MORE ABOUT HER STORY

"The Legacy of Florence Allshorn" by Eleanor Brown
(International Bulletin of Mission Research, vol. 1, issue 8: 1984)

9

GLADYS AYLWARD

The Little Woman Who Trusted God for the Impossible

Standing at only four feet ten inches tall, Gladys Aylward, "the little woman," had a heart for God and a determination to go to China and tell the people about the Lord she had learned to love. She never believed people who told her that the things she wanted to do were beyond her ability. What she did, however, was memorialized in *TIME* and *Reader's Digest* magazines as well as the movie *The Inn of the Sixth Happiness* featuring the Swedish actress Ingrid Bergman (though the Hollywood script did not accurately depict Gladys's simple and heroic life).

Gladys was born just after the turn of the century, in 1902, to a working-class family in England. After reading a book about China as a teenager, Gladys felt called to become a missionary to that country. Her first step in that direction was met with failure. She enrolled in a Bible School that trained students to be missionaries but was unable to pass her subjects with acceptable grades. In fact, she was asked to drop out and make room for someone more qualified. The school's director told her that she was not smart enough to learn Chinese, and, should she ever get to China, the people would not accept her.

Undaunted, Gladys found work as a maid and began saving money from the pittance of the salary she received. She then went to a railroad station ticket office and told the agent she wanted to buy a ticket to China. The agent laughed at her because the ticket cost much more than Gladys had. She then opened a savings account and began depositing small sums of money each time she was paid.

The day finally came when she had enough money to buy the one-way ticket from England, through Europe, Russia, and Siberia to China. She used her petticoat as an "inside suitcase," sewing in valuables that she didn't want stolen. On the train, she met a Dutch couple who, learning that she intended to go to China, told her, "We will pray for you every night at 9:00 o'clock for the rest of our lives." Gladys never saw the couple again, but would need their prayers far more than she realized.

Inside Russia, she was caught in the Bolshevik Revolution and kidnapped by men who wanted to make her a forced laborer. She narrowly escaped from their grasp by leaping to the deck of a ship as it was pulling away from the dock. Upon arrival in China, she couldn't find the elderly missionary she had planned to meet up with. She discovered that the missionary had actually moved to another village, a two-day mule ride into the mountains. Gladys hired a mule driver who took her to the village.

The missionary, Jeannie Lawson, then seventy-three years of age, was surprised to see her but welcomed her help. Gladys's first task was to prepare the ancient house Ms. Lawson lived in to accommodate mule drivers as a kind of makeshift inn. Those who stayed there were not only provided with hot meals but also with Bible stories and beds without fleas.

When Ms. Lawson died, Gladys found favor with the local mandarin, an important government administrator, who asked her to become a "foot inspector" for the Chinese government, which was striving to eliminate the age-old practice of binding the feet of baby girls. This allowed her to meet women and to share the gospel with them.

Gladys's tender heart prompted her to take in more than two hundred homeless children who were unwanted by parents but loved by her. She could never say no to those who suffered or were homeless or hungry, especially children. Her most notable achievement came as the Japanese invaded China in World War II, killing all in their path. Realizing that children would not be spared, Gladys led ninety-four children across the mountains of northern China, through two provinces. It was a nearly impossible feat, but with God's help, she did it. When the children were safe, Gladys, exhausted, fell into a coma and was hospitalized for two months.

Following a short visit back to the country of her birth, England, she returned to China and spent the rest of her life helping the Chinese, who called her "Ai-weh-deh" or "Virtuous One."

Takeaway Thought

Gladys Aylward did not let anything stop her from doing what the Lord wanted her to do. Are you relentless in achieving good things for God? Don't let anyone convince you that you're too weak or too small to finish a noble task.

MORE ABOUT HER STORY

Gladys Aylward: The Little Woman by Gladys Aylward with Christine Hunter (Moody Publishers, 1970)

10

MICHELLE RUETSCHLE

Encourager, Wife, Mother,
and Therapist

When the phone rang, Michelle Ruetschle was busy unpacking luggage for her family's two-month stay in the US. The year was 2010 and Michelle's husband Steve had just turned forty. He had been serving as the senior pastor of Union Church in Manila, Philippines for several years, and as they did each year, the Ruetschles had returned to the US to visit family and renew friendships. Michelle took the phone from her mother-in-law, not realizing that their world had just imploded. The phone message was short and brusque: Steve had been in an accident and he was being taken to the hospital. The message that something was wrong with his neck and they had to do immediate surgery seemed, in Michelle's words, "to stubbornly float above my consciousness, out of reach, afraid to land."

Steve had been riding a motorcycle ahead of his brother and when he navigated a curve, the motorcycle went out from under him. A few minutes later, his brother found Steve's crumpled body lying on the side of the road. When police finally arrived, they recognized that his condition was too precarious to endure an ambulance ride. He needed to be airlifted to a hospital. As he was being loaded onto a gurney, unable to move, he told his brother to tell his wife and the boys he loved them and asked that his brother take care of them for him.

With the diagnosis of a severed spinal cord, Steve was airlifted in a private jet to one of the finest rehab facilities in the US. The days that followed were horribly difficult. The boys didn't understand what was happening. Michelle had to find inner strength to cope with dark circumstances. She described the small room Steve was placed in at the rehabilitation facility, saying, "Apart from a hospital-issued bed, table, and closet, there was a large recliner in the corner of the room by the window. It folded out into what was almost a bed. This became my outpost, my place of reprieve, my corner residence."

Then the battle began—a challenge to their faith as doubts bombarded them both: Where was God when he could have kept this from happening? Would Steve ever recover? Michelle had found Jesus Christ through an InterVarsity group when she studied in Canada, but nothing had ever tested her faith as did Steve's accident.

She knew what the odds were. Her husband was declared to have quadriplegia and perhaps never recover.

Their future was dark. Michelle was fully aware of the odds of all this playing out in a positive fashion. Eventually, two people were able to prop up Steve to a sitting position. He then graduated to a wheelchair. Progress was slow. Not only did his body need healing, but his heart, mind, and faith needed restoration as well.

Michelle, an attorney by training, became an encourager and therapist as well as a wife and mother. She committed herself to hope when despair was staring her in the face. She clung to faith in the healing power of God when Steve's condition gave little evidence that anything positive was happening. God honored that hope and the prayers of many.

With Michelle's indefatigable support, Steve regained the ability to walk and resume his ministerial duties, although he still lives with pain. Having been in the fellowship of the wounded, he has become a more tenderhearted, understanding person who speaks from a heart of compassion. Michelle, reflecting on what she has gone through, wrote, "I looked back over the year and counted the cost. I honored a love grown thicker with adversity, more resilient with sacrifice, stronger with hardship."

As a friend of many years, I credit Michelle with being the conduit of God's grace that brought restoration and healing to her husband by living out the love of Jesus in unfathomable difficulty.

Takeaway Thought

It took incredible strength and faith for Michelle Ruetschle to hold on to hope in midst of her family's crisis. God held her steady when the ground below her began to shake. Is your family facing a storm right now? Continue to encourage each other until the sky clears.

MORE ABOUT HER STORY

Forty: The Year My Husband Became a Quadriplegic by Michelle Ruetschle (2016)

11

VIRGINIA PRODAN

The Woman Who Led Her Assassin to Christ

Henry Wadsworth Longfellow, the nineteenth century American poet, is credited with writing, "Though the mills of God grind slowly, yet they grind exceeding small; Though with patience He stands waiting, with exactness grinds he all." What he meant was that sooner or later, God's invisible but powerful hand of justice rights the injustices that have caused others to suffer.

On Christmas Day in 1989, the Romanian dictator Nicolae Ceausescu and his wife, Elena, were executed by a firing squad. The deaths of the despised couple ended a quarter-century of oppression and misery for most Romanians. Under his government, thousands of people were brutally tortured and executed. No individual, however, could have been more relieved than a woman who stands barely five feet tall, Virginia Prodan, one of Ceausescu's most hated persons.

Ceausescu had hated Virginia so much that he once hired an assassin to get rid of her. One day, a tall, muscular man wearing a dark coat came to her law office and demanded to see her. Virginia wondered if she might be another victim of the regime. When he entered her office, he closed the door behind him, and as their eyes met Virginia saw, in her own words, "a bloodthirsty yet wounded lion."[6] The man pulled back his coat and reached into a shoulder holster. Drawing his gun and releasing the safety, he said, "I've come here to finish the matter once and for all." And the chilling words followed, "I am here to kill you!"

Who was this woman, and how could she be so hated by the government but so loved and revered by many Christians? The story of her life is told in her book *Saving My Assassin*, one of the most compelling, totally captivating books I have ever read, and the short space in this selection can only touch upon the highlights of her life.

When Virginia was an infant she was given away, a fact that she painfully learned about many years afterward. She had her suspicions, though. Her flaming red hair set her apart from everyone in the family, and she was treated like a servant, not a daughter. In her senior year of high school, she passed the baccalaureate exam and was allowed to take an admission exam for law school. She was sent to Bucharest to stay with a gentle, caring woman she called

---

[6] Author interview (April 2017).

"Aunt Cassandra," who immediately bonded with Virginia. But Virginia's mother abruptly decided that Virginia could no longer live with Cassandra, and Virginia was forced to move into an abandoned dormitory with neither plumbing nor other basic amenities. (It was only years later, after Cassandra had passed away, that Virginia discovered that Cassandra was actually her birth mother!)

Now fast forward to many years later. Virginia became an attorney, and a man named Nestor came to her office wanting her to defend his parents whose house had been illegally seized. After observing Nestor's sense of inner peace, she casually said, "I wish I had what you have in your life." Taking his chance, he asked her, "Do you go to church?" "On Christmas and Easter," she replied. Nestor took Virginia and her children to his church, where the pastor quoted the words of Jesus in John 14:6: "I am the way and the truth and the life. No one comes to the Father except through me." This verse struck Virginia's heart like a bolt of lightning. She realized that Jesus was what she had been searching for all her life without realizing it. She was converted!

Virginia became a champion for Christians in court. Her knowledge of the law was impeccable. Her courage was daunting. Her able defense saved numerous churches from destruction and kept large numbers of pastors out of prison. Her success also made her an enemy of the government, which sought to silence her forever.

When she faced the assassin sent to kill her, the Spirit of God spoke to her, saying, "Share the gospel with this man!" Emboldened, she asked the would-be killer, "Have you ever asked yourself, 'Why do I exist?' or 'Why am I here?' or 'What is the meaning of life?'" Slowly, he began to listen to what Virginia was saying and, that evening, instead of killing her, he prayed the sinner's prayer with her! An assassin's dark heart was enlightened.

Ronald Reagan eventually granted a political asylum visa to Virginia and her family, who moved to Dallas, Texas. Years later, she once again met her assassin—but not in a closed room or dark alley. Having gone to seminary, he was serving a church in the United States as the pastor! Unbelievable? Yes! God is full of surprises as this dynamic woman who ranks among the bravest of the brave would tell you.

Takeaway Thought

Talk about courage! Virginia Prodan stared death in the face and didn't even flinch. In that crucial moment, she was more concerned about her assassin's spiritual condition than her own life. Are you just as passionate and committed to share the gospel with others? Trust the Holy Spirit to give you the courage and the right words to say when the time comes to be bold.

MORE ABOUT HER STORY

Saving My Assassin by Virginia Prodan
(Tyndale House, 2016)

12

MOTHER TERESA

A Saint among the Dying

Though she was born in what is now the Republic of North Macedonia, the entire world is in Mother Teresa's debt. When she was born on August 26, 1910, she was named Agnes Gonxha Bojaxhiu. Her father died when she was seven years old and her mother was forced to start a business selling embroidered cloth. Her brother, determined to do something with his life that would lift him from poverty, enlisted in the army and became an officer. When his eighteen-year-old sister decided to become a missionary, he chided her, saying, "Why don't you make something of your life?" For many years, their relationship was broken. How could he have known then that his sister would someday stand among admirers in Norway to receive the Nobel Prize for her work with the poor? No other woman has touched the lives of so many suffering, hurting people in her lifetime than this woman.

Taking the name Sister Teresa, honoring Saints Teresa of Lisieux and Teresa of Avila, she cultivated a powerful faith that believed identifying with the poorest of the poor is really to identify with Jesus, who had nothing but a hand-woven garment that soldiers gambled for when he was crucified. Lady Jordan, a British woman of significant influence and wealth, asked Sister Teresa, "How can you touch a leper and smile?" Sister Teresa replied, "I know that when I touch the limbs of a leper, I am touching the body of Christ." It was said that Sister Teresa didn't look at people collectively, but she looked at one face, smile, heart at a time.

Sister Teresa also had a fierce belief that every person is important to our Heavenly Father—the baby girl resting on the top of an overflowing garbage bin, the fifty thousand lepers in India, the runaway, the unloved teenager, and the hungry and homeless person who was dying. Those who worked with her would often hear her assessment of a great need with the words, "God will provide!" even though she had nothing but a simple faith. And God honored her faith. She saw many of her prayers answered.

These few paragraphs are hopelessly inadequate to describe her courage in breaking ranks with a culture that whispers, "The poor are worthless, the dying are not worth the bother, you can't make a difference." When the situation demanded it, Mother Teresa could be as tough as nails. At a prayer breakfast in Washington, D.C., she singled out President Bill Clinton, who was sitting a few feet away from her, and rebuked him for his position on abortion, which she considered to be murder.

She told her biographer, Navin Chawla, "We are called upon not to be successful but to be faithful," and faithful she was, even unto death. When her light was finally extinguished on September 5, 1997, more than four thousand members of the missionary organization she founded carried on her work.

When she was honored by receiving the prestigious Nobel Prize in 1979, she reluctantly went to Oslo, Norway. In her acceptance speech she said, "Personally, I am unworthy. I accept in the name of the poor, because I believe that by giving me the prize the committee is recognizing the presence of the poor in the world."[7]

A few moments later she said, "It is not enough for us to say, 'I love God,' but I also have to love my neighbor. The Apostle John says you are a liar if you say you love God and you don't love your neighbor."

Jesus said, "Whenever you did one of these things to someone overlooked or ignored, that was me—you did it to me" (Matthew 25:40 MSG). At Mother Teresa's death, India's president, K. R. Narayanan, said, "Such a one as she rarely walks upon this earth!" And it may well be that even in heaven there are few who have touched the lives of so many suffering people on earth as Mother Teresa.

---

[7] D. Jeanene Watson, *Teresa of Calcutta* (Mott Media, 1984), 158.

Takeaway Thought

Are there marginalized people around you? Is there somebody who needs a touch from Jesus? Be like Mother Teresa and extend your caring hand to those who are craving to know that they are loved.

MORE ABOUT HER STORY

Mother Teresa: The Authorized Biography
by Navin Chawla (Element Books, 1996)

13

GERTRUDE CHAMBERS

The Woman Who Made Her Husband's Name a Household Name

Walk into just about any Christian bookstore, anywhere in the world, and you will find something authored by an early twentieth-century Scottish Bible teacher named Oswald Chambers. His book *My Utmost for His Highest* has become the world's best-selling devotional book, translated into many languages. Yet had it not been for Gertrude Chambers, the little known and unrecognized driving force behind his writings, very few people today would even know the name Oswald Chambers.

Gertrude's name never appeared in or on any of the fifty books which bear the name of her husband. In the foreword to *My Utmost for His Highest*, she wrote about how the selections had come from various speaking engagements, yet she signed only with the initials, "B. D." And what did "B. D." represent? In her book *Searching for Mrs. Oswald Chambers*, Martha Christian explains that "B. D." was short for "Beloved Disciple." And quickly pronounced, the letters B. D., sounded like "Biddy," a term of affection her husband called her (not bearing the negative connotation the term has acquired in our day).

What is the story of the remarkable woman who remained entirely hidden behind the work of her husband? Before his death in 1917, a few of Oswald Chambers's sermons had been published and distributed to the soldiers that he had ministered to. Some of them had been printed as booklets, but not a single book had gone to press. Chambers was ministering to British troops in Egypt when he died suddenly as a result of complications following an appendectomy. His untimely death at the age of forty-three was mourned by thousands of people. So well-loved was he by the men he ministered to that despite not being part of the military, he was given a full military burial in the old British cemetery in Cairo. At his funeral, battle-hardened soldiers wept over the passing of the gangly Scotsman.

Oswald and Gertrude had been married for just seven years. And at the age of thirty-four, she had become a widow and the single mother of a little girl. After Oswald was buried, Gertrude was sitting outside their home in Zeitoun, Egypt, reading Oswald's Bible when a young man dressed in his military uniform approached. He fumbled with his hat as he asked her, "How will we go on without a teacher?" That conversation triggered the understanding that she was the one to carry on her husband's work.

Gertrude and her small daughter returned to England, where her efforts made her husband's writing available to countless thousands. Before she met Oswald, Gertrude had become a stenographer. She could write shorthand faster than people could talk, and from the time she first began listening to her husband's messages, she had taken shorthand notes, hundreds of them—never thinking that one day they would be transcribed to become the texts of his books, and that she would become the editor as well as publisher of many of them.

If you have been blessed by the writings of Oswald Chambers as I have been over the years, you will agree that the Christian world owes a tremendous debt of gratitude to this humble and gracious woman whose gargantuan efforts have touched so many.

In today's "me centered" social media culture, it seems strange for anyone to devote herself to editing and publishing someone else's works. Yet Gertrude Chambers wanted it that way. She believed that in Oswald's writings, people would see Christ. As biographer David McCasland comments, it was "their utmost for God's highest."

Takeaway Thought

How important are fame and recognition to you? If you were given the chance to do something great but remain relatively unknown, would you do it? Gertrude Chambers did, and the world has been incredibly blessed by her dedication and hard work. We might not get our reward here on earth, but we will in heaven someday.

MORE ABOUT HER STORY

Searching for Mrs. Oswald Chambers
by Martha Christian (Tyndale House, 2008)

Oswald Chambers: Abandoned to God
by David McCasland (Discovery House, 1998)

14

MARY SLESSOR

Everybody's Mother

Mary Slessor, the second of seven children, was born in 1848 to poor parents. Her childhood was marred by family strife and the outbursts of her father's anger. When alcohol finally overcame him, the scant wages of her mother drove the family to Dundee, Scotland, where young Mary grew up. It was a tough world for this red-headed, street-wise girl who dropped out of school at age eleven to work alongside her mother in a textile mill. By the time she was fourteen, she was working full time in the mill as her mother was confined to their home with the birth of a seventh child. For the next thirteen years Mary worked full time to support her family. At the same time, she became involved in a local Presbyterian Church and was active in a street mission.

Then Mary heard that one of her heroes, missionary David Livingstone, another Scot, had died kneeling by his bed. Her heart was touched. Mary's two brothers had both felt called to be missionaries to Africa but died before their plans materialized. Her biographers are in agreement that the girl who knew how to use her knuckles with the local rowdies had a tender heart, and when she heard a missionary to Africa speak, Mary was set on fire to become a missionary herself.

Hearing that the Calabar Mission in West Africa would enlist women, Mary applied and was accepted as a missionary at the age of twenty-seven. After spending her first few years at a mission station, she quickly picked up the language. However, she never felt quite at home. After the death of her mother and sister, Mary began to feel closer to heaven than to Britain, and there was no longer anything keeping her from pushing further into the interior of Africa. Mary went to an Africa that was reeling from the horrors of the slave trade. She fought cultural injustices. In spite of bouts with malaria that sapped her strength, Mary decided she would always go where she was needed.

Mary never opposed African traditions because they were not European. She was opposed, however, to practices that degraded the Africans themselves, and especially women, who were often abused and considered property. When she felt an injustice was taking place, she threatened and begged those in power in order to save lives. She learned that when twins were born, one or both were killed—the result of a belief that one had been fathered by the devil. She would find the mothers of these twins and do everything she could to rescue one or both of the infants. She adopted dozens of babies left to die in the bush. She fought for the right of African women to be free from the threat of being put to death at the whim of their husbands. For nearly forty years, she lived in a village hut. She not only survived where others had failed because of the severity of the climate and culture, but she flourished, convinced that a single woman could go places men could not go and understand the needs of women as only a woman could.

Because of her strength of personality and character, she became not only respected but loved by the people of Calabar. Her reputation as a peacemaker spread. She became an arbitrator and served as the first vice-consul of Okoyong, Nigeria, a government position she held for many years. Mary's strength was that she thought as a native, lived as one, and sought to bring her faith to bear on their needs.

When Mary died and word of her homegoing spread, the cry went out: "Eka Kpukpro Quo," meaning, "Everybody's mother is dead!" Thousands wept over the loss of the woman who is among the greatest of Christian missionaries in the nineteenth century.

Takeaway Thought

Mary Slessor enthusiastically accepted the living conditions, customs, and hardships of those she sought to serve. In many ways, she followed the example of Jesus, who came down from heaven and lived among us as a man. What will it take for us to adopt the same attitude if we want to relate to and serve people of all backgrounds? What can you can do to alleviate the suffering happening around you?

MORE ABOUT HER STORY

Mary Slessor: A Life on the Altar of God
by Bruce McLennan (Christian Focus, 2014)

15

LILLIAN TRASHER

The Nile Mother of Egypt

Although she never gave birth to a child of her own, over 8,000 orphans—the children of Muslims, Christians, and folk religionists—called Lillian Trasher "Mother." To Lillian, they were simply babies who desperately needed food, clothing, a place to sleep, and, as much as anything else, a mother's love. She gave them exactly what they needed.

Lillian Hunt Trasher, born on September 27, 1887 in Florida, was raised by Quaker parents who were opposed to war and bearing arms. She was still in her teens when she attended Bible college, and then for several years, she worked at an orphanage. Lillian spent these years finding her purpose and calling in life. After she failed to get satisfying employment following her time at the orphanage, she became engaged to a minister. But there was a problem. She was conflicted when she sensed that she was called to be a missionary in Africa, but her husband-to-be didn't share that calling. Ten days before the wedding was to take place, amidst many tears, Lillian broke the engagement. Then, for a short period of time, she taught in another Bible school and traveled as part of an evangelistic team. She even pastored a Pentecostal church, but her heart was again drawn to the orphanage where she had previously worked. She returned to minister to the children.

At a missionary conference, Lillian heard an Egyptian pastor describe the needs in Africa and the Spirit of God seemed to impress upon her that this is where she should serve. Her parents were strongly opposed to her even thinking of going to Egypt, realizing that she would be far, far away from home and the security of a familiar environment. She respected her parents' wishes, but she felt God speaking to her every time she read the account of his words to Moses: "I have indeed seen the oppression of my people in Egypt. ... I have come down to set them free. Now come, I will send you back to Egypt" (Acts 7:34). Those words burned in her heart, and she interpreted them as God telling her, "Egypt is where I want you!"

Shortly thereafter, Lillian, accompanied by her sister Jennie, sailed to Egypt with less than $100 between them. But she wasn't worried about surviving on such a small amount because she had a firm conviction that if God sent her there, he would provide for her, as he had provided for missionaries like Hudson Taylor in China and George Müeller in Britain.

The two sisters settled into a mission compound in Assiout, about 230 miles south of Cairo. Soon after their arrival, a man came searching for someone who could provide care for his dying wife. Lillian went to the bedside of the man's wife. The woman died soon after they arrived, but left behind a tiny baby girl. When the baby's grandmother revealed that she was planning to throw the sick child into the Nile, Lillian was indignant. She gave the baby the name Fareida and took her back to the mission compound with her.

Other nearly starving children were soon brought to the mission headquarters, and two years later the count was some fifty orphaned children along with ten homeless widows. When Britain expelled all foreigners from Egypt during a period of civil unrest, Lillian briefly returned to the US, where she told the story of the needs in Egypt and how her heart was burdened to feed the hungry, love the homeless children, and provide a place of refuge for the suffering and afflicted.

Finding financial and prayer support in Assembly of God Churches, she returned to Egypt for the next fifty years, ministering non-stop without a single furlough. She endured Nazi occupation during World War II and earned a reputation as "The Nile Mother of Egypt." Before she died in 1961, more than 1,200 children were being fed in the orphanages where she worked. Her work was supported by groups as varied as the Presbyterian Churches of Egypt, the Soul Salvation Society, and churches in the United States. Today, the work that she birthed is continued and recognized by even more groups and organizations. She is honored by the Episcopal Church in the United States, which designates a feast day in her honor on their liturgical calendar for December 19. When Lillian breathed her first taste of celestial air on December 17, 1961, she was buried in her orphanage's cemetery in accord with Egyptian law. A generation of men and women, now serving in many capacities, have risen to call her "blessed!"

In her generation, women missionaries were often thought of as "second-class servants," but Mother Lillian Trasher proved that the voice of God heard distinctly through the cry of a destitute, hungry, suffering child is all that one needs to accomplish what not even respected men could do.

Takeaway Thought

Lillian Trasher helped save the lives of thousands of children because she heeded the call of God to care for them. Is God calling you to do something for the weak, the helpless, and the powerless?

16

AUNTIE WANG

The Woman Who Was Alone but Not Lonely

Deborah Wang, a frail but vibrant saint, endured what no woman should ever have to face. Her husband, Wang Ming Dao, was one of the unofficial architects of the house church movement in China. After the Chinese Revolution of 1949, the communist government began converting church buildings into warehouses, and pastors were imprisoned or forced to go underground. Children were taken into the homes of family or friends. Deborah's husband had said, "They can close the churches (referring to buildings) but they cannot stop us from worshiping in homes." For that, he was arrested and imprisoned. Then she, too, was imprisoned for being involved in "anti-revolutionary" activities. For twenty years, she faced the bitter cold of northern Chinese winters with thin clothing and insufficient food in prison.

I met the Wangs for the first time in 1989. I'll never forget the afternoon I sat in their humble little apartment in Shanghai and listened to them recount their experiences. I was drawn to the strength of this saintly woman whose smile came from her heart. As she talked about the years of imprisonment, I asked, "Did you ever lose hope?" After all, twenty years of separation from a loved one, with very little news and few letters, is a very long time. Her eyes spoke far more than her words as she quietly answered, "No, never."

After the Wangs were released from prison, their home became a refuge for those who needed encouragement and counsel. Only God knows how many cups of tea Auntie Wang (as her friends called her) served to weary men and women who made their way up the stairs to her flat.

Two weeks after her husband passed away at the age of ninety-one, I again visited Auntie Wang. The ashes of her late husband were in an urn on the table behind the chair which Brother Wang had used as a pulpit to share God's Word. A friend and I sought to comfort her, quoting some favorite passages of Scripture. But it was Auntie Wang who really encouraged and comforted us.

"Auntie Wang," I said, "I will pray that you will not be lonely." Pausing for just a moment, she spoke with a clear and resolute tone of voice, "I will not be lonely. I was not lonely before." It was what she didn't say that spoke the loudest. That word, *before*, not only included the fact that she had seen her husband only three times during their twenty years of imprisonment, but also the fact that both she and her husband had paid the price of hunger, suffering, and privation for their commitment to the Lord.

That word, *before,* rang in my ears again when a close friend told how Deborah Wang had developed pneumonia and was taken to a Shanghai hospital. With no rooms available, she was given a temporary bed in a hallway, and there in the early hours of the morning on April 18, 1992, she met the God who had been her companion for so many years. As the leaves of the trees were budding, following the cold of a Shanghai winter, Deborah Wang made her entrance into the presence of the Lord where a faithful and devoted husband awaited her, a place where rivers never freeze and flowers never fade, a place where the word *good-bye* is never spoken.

I was saddened that she couldn't be surrounded by friends and flowers when the angel sweetly took her hand and escorted her across the threshold of heaven. But I am sure of one fact: While she was alone, she was not lonely. She had the promise of her Lord, who said, "And behold, I am with you always" (Matthew 28:20 ESV). Deborah Wang experienced that, both in life and in death.

Takeaway Thought

Do you ever feel lonely? When you think that your family and friends have deserted you, remember that God promised in Hebrews 13:5, "I will never leave you nor forsake you" (NKJV). Deborah Wang learned about this promise and took it to heart until the Lord called her home.

17

EVANGELINE BOOTH

The Woman Who Knew Who She Truly Was

It's been said that over a thousand men proposed to her during her lifetime. She had offers from millionaires, farmers, businessmen, fishermen, and vagrants from the Bowery. She was not an actress or a movie star, but she had a tremendous following of 38,000 people who became ambassadors of goodwill in eighty-six countries. Her name was Evangeline Booth and she headed the Salvation Army.

Born in London in 1865, she was the seventh of eight children born to William Booth and Catherine Mumford, who had earlier founded the Christian mission that became the Salvation Army. At fifteen, Evangeline was a Sergeant distributing the Salvation Army's paper, *The War Cry*, in the slums of east London. At the age of twenty-one, she became an officer. When there was trouble somewhere, her father would say, "Send Evangeline!" She served with the Salvation Army in the US and then in Canada, and then returned to the US where she held the top position of leadership.

When World War I erupted, she led a small "army" of Salvationists to the trenches of France, where they soon won the favor of troops with what was described as their "cheerful brand of 'seven-days-a-week Christianity.'" They served as nurses, relief workers, and taught Bible classes for the troops. The Salvation Army was able to raise $13 million to support the troops abroad—a very sizable amount for that day! It was under Evangeline's leadership that the Salvation Army was firmly established as a humanitarian outreach, touching the lives of suffering people wherever they were.

Throughout her life, she was a tremendous administrator, musician, and friend to thousands. When she was interviewed by a reporter, she said that her secret was this: "I live for others. My deepest desire is to make every person I meet a little better because I have passed this way."

What truly distinguished Evangeline from her contemporaries? First—her generosity. She gave of herself without reservation, without thought of what she got in return. The second was her genuineness. She was authentic and unpretentious. Her clothes or her looks were never what left an impression on people. She was remembered as someone who radiated warmth and care. Third, she had strong convictions and refused to take the path of least resistance. For a young man or woman to join the Salvation Army in Evangeline Booth's day meant they were willing to commit to a life of simplicity and to pledge to engage in spiritual warfare. The fourth quality that set Evangeline apart was her desire to please God rather than herself. She often quoted the words of Paul: "Am I now seeking the approval of man, or of God? Or am I trying to please man? If I were still trying to please man, I would not be a servant of Christ" (Galatians 1:10 ESV).

I have a deep respect and admiration for those who have outgrown the platitudes of their contemporaries and refuse to let the world force them into its mold. May God give us more people who, like Evangeline Booth, are committed to the cause of touching the lives of those around them.

Takeaway Thought

What motivates you to get up every day? Think about a cause greater than what will only give you worldly success. Evangeline Booth remained a committed soldier of God's army and no doubt she heard God when he welcomed her to heaven, "Well done, good and faithful servant" (Matthew 25:23).

MORE ABOUT HER STORY

When Others Shuddered: Eight Women Who Refused to Give Up by Jamie Janosz (Moody Publishers, 2014)

18
TRUDY KIM

The "Invisible" Servant of the Lord

When Trudy packed her suitcase to go away to college in Greenville, South Carolina, never in her wildest dreams did she have any idea of what lay ahead of her. At school, she fell in love with a young man who was from Korea, knew little English, and would someday preach to tens of thousands. His name is Billy Kim, and Trudy's story is inseparably interwoven with his.

When Billy proposed to Trudy, her parents somewhat reluctantly gave their blessing to the marriage, realizing that their daughter would probably live and raise her family in a land that had been ravaged by war. Upon arriving in Korea in 1959, Billy took Trudy to his family home—a simple Korean farmhouse that was sparsely heated by dangerous charcoal blocks stuffed into tubes under the floor. The introduction to a new culture was less than pleasant. Trudy learned that it was a custom for Korean men to be fed first, while the women ate what was left. She spoke only a few phrases of the language and was not always accepted by Koreans, who pointed out the fact her eyes were a different color and her complexion was light.

Every day was a new experience as she picked up a few more Korean words and learned from her mother-in-law how to cook Korean food and how to navigate the culture. While Trudy's Korean was less than perfect, she spoke the language of love—a powerful language that crosses all barriers. When I interviewed her daughter, Mary Kay Park, and asked about her earliest childhood memory, she replied, "There wasn't a lot of food in our home, yet the lack was never felt. Somehow God always provided and mom was very resourceful in finding ways to stretch the food that we did have." For example, she used the powdered milk sent from America to make ice milk or milk popsicles.

When Trudy saw a need, she quietly set about to meet that need. When someone had no place to sleep, she invited the person to sleep at the Kim house. When her husband started a church and there were no restaurants nearby, she invited people to her home after the service, and they came by the dozens without Trudy knowing exactly how many will be sitting down to eat. But, somehow, there was always just enough food served with a smile and an American flavor.

In 1994, after seeing the need for Christian training and academic excellence, Trudy became the moving force that founded a day school. Within a few short months, the school was widely acclaimed for its academic excellence as well as its commitment to Christian values. For this, Trudy was awarded two honorary doctorate degrees. When she learned that Koreans liked American-style pies, she began baking pies and selling them for a small amount, using the proceeds to fund a program for special needs children at the school.

"How will you remember your mother?" I asked Mary Kay, and she replied that her mother had the gift of "invisible servant leadership." Trudy's style of leadership was not seeking the limelight, not even intentionally "leading, but quietly making a difference in the lives of needy people."

Her actions spoke to the needs and hearts of people. In the spirit of Jesus, who washed the feet of the disciples, Trudy did what was needed, regardless of what it was. The way in which she impacted her family, her culture, and her world is reflected in Galatians 2:20 which reads, "My old self has been crucified with Christ. It is no longer I who live, but Christ who lives in me. So I live in this earthly body by trusting in the Son of God, who loved me and gave himself for me" (Galatians 2:20 NLT).

The generous and caring nature that Trudy developed is indeed rare. In the status-driven culture in which she lived, Trudy treated everyone around her equally. She spent her life putting others first, doing what needed to be done.

In 1973, Billy Graham came to Korea and Trudy's husband was his translator as he spoke to more than a million people. This brought a stream of international guests that Trudy ministered to. Billy Kim was also instrumental in founding the Far East Broadcasting Company's station on Jeju Island, and with his growing recognition, more people visited the country and were touched by Trudy's care and generosity. May we all be inspired to act with "invisible servant leadership!"

Takeaway Thought

Do you live only to hear the applause of people and the praise of others? Trudy Kim didn't have the spotlight on her while she served God and people, but she willingly served anyway. You might be an "invisible" servant on earth, but you and your good works will always be visible to God.

19

FLORENCE LIN

The Unwelcomed Infant Who Became a "Can-Do!" Adult

When Florence Lin returned to China, the land of her birth, for ministry, she was invited to speak in a house church to a group of women. Florence was enjoying her time as more and more people arrived late and stood in the back of the group. But when someone began shouting, "Stop! Stop!" things quickly took a turn for the worse. Everyone was arrested and taken into custody by the police. Florence was interrogated and accused of committing a crime against the government because she spoke about God. Only after signing a confession that she was guilty of a crime was she allowed to have enough food to avoid going into diabetic shock, a condition she suffered from. She was kept overnight at the police station and released with instructions not to speak publicly. As harrowing as this experience was, even more challenging was her flashbacks to her childhood experiences.

Florence was born in Canton, now known as Guangzhou, during the early days of World War II. Her birth was not celebrated by her family, who had wanted a son. Her father was a double agent, working for both the Japanese as well as the Chinese, something that eventually resulted in the entire family's being arrested and imprisoned by the Japanese while Florence was still a small child. Even today, as a woman in her eighties, she cannot forget hearing the screams of those who were tortured by the Japanese in the room adjacent to where her family was kept.

Eventually, the war ended, and although her father was strongly opposed to Christianity, he put Florence in a Christian school because it was the best education available. The family then moved to Taiwan, where as a teenager, Florence clearly heard the gospel. When her parents who were devout Buddhists learned that she had converted to Christianity, they threw her out of the house. The missionary couple who had led her to Christ helped her find employment at a Christian student center.

Florence was on her own. But she had confidence that God would provide for her. The house where she was living had no central heating, and her feet would turn black from the cold. She prayed for shoes despite not knowing where they would come from. On Christmas Eve, a box appeared on her bed with a pair of green shoes inside with a note that says that the pair could be exchanged for another—something that normally was never done in China.

About a year after Florence's conversion, a young man named John Lin began coming to the center where she worked, and soon the two got acquainted. John eventually proposed to Florence. She joined him in Okinawa where he worked as a civil engineer. Unable to find a Chinese church, the couple went to a chapel where they met two missionaries with the Far East Broadcasting Company (FEBC)—a missionary enterprise that would play a significant part in their lives for many years.

As the first Chinese missionaries to work with FEBC, John and Florence used their skills in a variety of ways. Soon the Lins founded a Chinese church that grew along with their family. When the FEBC went on the air, Florence began producing Christian radio programs beamed into China. At first there was no response. Nonetheless, the Lins continued to proclaim the gospel by faith. It was years before the "Bamboo Curtain" was lifted and they learned that literally thousands of men and women had been listening.

Eventually, John and Florence were sent to Singapore, where they established an office for the FEBC, and labored there for ten years before returning to the US. When John retired, the Lins founded Joy Partners, an organization focused on ministry to China. When God called John home to be in heaven, Florence continued and expanded the ministry, partnering with ChiLin Huang, a talented musician, and his wife, Rachel.

Florence continued to do everything to serve the Lord. For instance, together with her ministry partners, she taught church members how to play the keyboard and provided financial assistance for village pastors and children in China. She also gave money management training to young couples in the US and produced numerous albums of Chinese music. Seeing the needs of small children in rural areas of China, she started "To Village with Love," a ministry that provided clothing and food for children in neglected areas.

The infant who was unwelcomed because she was a girl had an appointment with destiny. She grew to become a strong "can-do" woman who persevered through hardship to do whatever God called her to accomplish—with a song and a smile.

Takeaway Thought

Do you think that life dealt you a bad deck of cards when you were born? Instead of being bitter about not having the best family background, ask God to help you rise above your difficult circumstances the way Florence Lin did. Don't let anything keep you from being the best you can be for God's glory.

20

DR. KIM PASCUAL

Living Out the Love of Jesus

She was abandoned by her mother when she was just two weeks old. Though she grew up in an adoptive Christian home, she never really understood salvation until the evening before she was to have her first cancer surgery. She understands loneliness, pain, and suffering because she has experienced the same thing. She has been responsible for providing medical care, education, water wells, and restroom facilities for countless thousands of people in distress.

Who is this mostly unrecognized but saintly woman?

Most babies in our world are welcomed by a loving mother and a doting father. Some, however, are merely considered "unwanted cargo" to be disposed of one way or another, whether it is by abortion or abandonment. When Kim Pascual came into the world, it was abandonment. Two weeks after she was born in the 1950s in the Island Nation of the Philippines, her birth mother left her father and child for another man. Her father fought for custody of the baby and provided a loving environment where baby Kim grew up with an aunt who adopted her.

Realizing that medical doctors are generally well compensated for their services, Kim's aunt urged her to consider medicine as a career. She enrolled in a university with a biology major as a prerequisite to being admitted to medical school. During her senior year in the university, Kim was diagnosed with cancer and given no more than five years to live. She recounts, "I then thought, 'Why wait for death? Live a normal life, and if I die, I die!'"[8]

Following surgery for the cancer, she endured radiation as she began classes in medical school. Two years after graduating from medical school, she was again diagnosed with cancer. Instead of surgery, however, the Great Physician, Jesus Christ, healed her again. Knowing that the God who heals had touched her, she longed even more strongly to bring healing to the needy and dedicated her life to touching others with hope and healing, as God would open a door for her.

She found the open door in 1994 when Gordon Robertson (Host of Christian Broadcasting Network's *700 Club*) came to the Philippines and made contact with Dr. Kim. He asked her to be involved with the ministry Operation Blessing Philippines. Operation Blessing is a humanitarian organization that brings medical care, clean water, and disaster and hunger relief to suffering communities throughout the world. Dr. Kim was asked

---

[8] Author interview (November 2019).

to head all medical outreach for the Philippines and coordinate the work of the Operation Blessing Hospital Airplane. It was the beginning of a long and rich lifetime of service.

When I moved to the Philippines in 1974, an area outside Manila had begun to gain notoriety and was called Smokey Mountain. Some thirty thousand people lived atop a garbage dump, daily sifting through the two million metric tons of waste and garbage, consuming anything that was edible and suffering physically from exposure to disease-causing organisms and toxic fumes from the burning garbage. Dr. Kim provided medical care to all that she could, undaunted by the stench and utter horror of the slum. This was only one of many areas that would be transformed by Dr. Kim and Operation Blessing.

Besides medical care, Operation Blessing was able to assist the garbage-picking families by feeding their children and assisting the families financially so that they could educate their children. Dr. Kim believes that providing resources, which includes helping the children get an education, is part of the rehabilitation necessary to lead a normal, productive life. She tells stories of changed lives: one of the boys helped by Operation Blessing is now a teacher; another grew up to own a piggery business and is a pastor; while a third is now a supervisor in an automobile manufacturing plant; a young woman who had been raped worked through her pain and is now working with a non-government agency helping others find hope and healing.

While Dr. Kim has made a tremendous difference in the lives of thousands as a doctor addressing the physical needs of people and a first responder providing crisis assistance in numerous Asian countries, she provides not only medical help and material assistance, but also a powerful dose of encouragement towards spiritual wellness. She leads people to experience physical healing and spiritual healing as well. She often lays hands on suffering people and prays for divine healing. When asked to recount some of these, she responded by telling the story of a woman who had been bedridden for three years. After Dr. Kim prayed for her, the woman got out of bed and walked. Another individual was blind and received sight, and a third was deaf and is now able to hear.

I am reminded of the story of a young man who was walking along a beach and began picking up starfish which had been stranded by a high tide, throwing them back into the ocean. A bystander commented, "You can't make a difference by doing that!" His response was, "It makes a difference to the ones I save!" So is it with Dr. Kim. She makes a difference—a big difference—with those whose lives are touched by her caring hands.

Takeaway Thought

Kim Pascual experienced firsthand what it meant to be miraculously healed by God. After committing herself to him, she became confident that our lives are in his hands. She is investing her life to help the poor, the sick, and the suffering. People are experiencing the love of Jesus through her. May the same thing be said about you as you relate with others every day.

21

MIRIAM NEFF

The Friend of Widows

When Mary anointed the feet of Jesus, he affirmed, "She has done what she could" (Mark 14:8 ESV). The same could be said of Miriam Neff, who lived in the shadow of her husband Bob for many years, as he served with Moody Bible Institute and managed their radio stations and related ministries in the 1960s and 70s. Early in their marriage, Miriam trusted Christ as her savior after seeing the Lord's presence in Bob's life. Miriam writes, "I became a believer through reading 1 John and observing the godly life of my husband. This was the most impactful decision of my life."[9]

In addition to raising four children, she began applying what she had learned in the classroom as well as from walking with the Lord to her employment as a professional high school counselor. On one occasion, a teenaged student came to her explaining she was pregnant and was considering an abortion. "Have you considered

---

[9] "Miriam Neff," Widow Connection: *http://widowconnection.com/about-miriam* (accessed March 9, 2018).

placing the baby for adoption?" Miriam inquired. "Only if you will tell my mother," she replied. Miriam met with the girl and her parents, and urged them to consider adoption rather than an abortion. They decided on adoption, and six months later, Miriam received a photo of the baby and on the back of the photo was the message, "If it were not for you, I would not be here!"

Miriam was salt and light in the school system for about twenty-six years, but that changed in the year 2006 when her husband passed away. Family friends abruptly became strangers. Long-time acquaintances never called, excusing their behavior by saying, "We wanted to give you some space." Many of the couples Miriam and her husband had known simply disappeared. Life was hard without a companion to share it with.

Experiencing the emptiness that often comes to a widow, Miriam began reaching out to other widows. During the first year of her widowhood, she went to Burkina Faso, Africa where she spoke to two hundred widows. She learned that when the women she met became widows, their lives changed in many ways far more painful than her own experience of loss. An African widow might lose her children, who were usually given to family members and treated as little more than slaves. If a widow was able to go with the children, she would be reduced to being "house help" or, in some cases, might be forced to turn to prostitution to provide for her children.

Her property would revert to a brother of the deceased, and she would have no freedom to choose what happened to her.

Miriam's heart was touched and she began a ministry to widows that has taken her into many countries of the world. How has she helped drive back the darkness? With the understanding that a marketable skill is key to independence and survival, her ministry began providing sewing machines for widows, as well as other measures to help widows become independent. While some organizations would give widows money with which to start businesses and required the widows to purchase their own equipment, Miriam felt this put too much pressure on widows and simply provided them with the sewing machines. Her humanitarian outreach to widows includes sponsoring sewing projects for widows in Africa and also in Albania.

Having a master's degree in counseling and years of professional experience (twenty-three years as a school counselor, three years as a teacher in high school, and two years in a university), Miriam went to her computer and began a career writing. Her eleven books speak to the needs of widows as only a widow can understand. She also found her voice as a spokeswoman for the needs of widows, establishing a non-profit organization known as Widow Connection, and produces a one-minute radio feature heard on over twelve hundred outlets.

When I asked her, "What is unique about your ministry?" she emphatically replied, "Nobody is doing it!" Hopefully, this will change as others understand the needs of widows whose lives are drastically altered following the death of a husband. May there be many more ministries like hers that provide not only the necessities of life but the love and care that only come with a hug and emotional support.

Takeaway Thought

Do you know someone whose life has seemingly fallen apart and they have no idea where to go in the circumstance they find themselves in? Reach out to them like Miriam Neff did and provide support. You can show love by helping them financially, through practical acts of service, or simply give them the gift of your presence, letting them talk, or not.

MORE ABOUT HER STORY

From One Widow to Another: Conversations on the New You by Mariam Neff (Moody Publishers, 2009)

22

GRACIA BURNHAM

Surviving 376 Days of Hell on Earth

The morning after she was rescued from spending over a year in captivity by the Abu Sayyaf terrorists in the Philippines, Gracia Burnham turned to her favorite passage in the Bible: "Therefore, since through God's mercy we have this ministry, we do not lose heart" (2 Corinthians 4:1). The word which the apostle Paul used, translated as "to lose heart," is found only three times in the New Testament. It means "to give up hope" or "to be discouraged."

Actually, that word described how Gracia felt, enduring 376 days and nights in the jungle, suffering through seventeen firefights as her captors battled the Philippine military, skimming the bugs and slime from the filthy water she drank, and watching her husband Martin slowly starving to death. In her book, *In the Presence of My Enemies*, Gracia very candidly tells of the struggles she fought with her emotions as well as her faith.

Gracia's hope to be rescued grew dimmer day by day. Lack of food and sleep, constant lies from her captors, and physical anguish did battle with her faith. Simply put, Gracia was mad at God for letting this happen. She writes, "I could hear Satan laughing at me, saying, 'You trust in the Lord—but you're still here.'" She told Martin, "I haven't given up my faith—I'm just choosing not to believe the part about God loving me. Because God's not coming through."

Finally, Gracia came to a crossroad, the same one that millions who have faced difficulty and hardship have confronted: Either you go with your emotions and turn your back on God, or you hold on to what you know is true regardless of circumstances. "I knew that I had a choice," she wrote. "I could give in to my resentment and allow it to dig me into a deeper and deeper hole both psychologically and emotionally, or I could choose to believe what God's Word says to be true whether I felt it was or not."

When she made that decision, it was a turning point for her. It enabled her to endure the terrible ordeal she faced. The rescue that saved her resulted in the death of the other two remaining hostages—her husband Martin and Ediborah Yap, a nurse.

Gracia's story is but another chapter in the ongoing spiritual battles for the souls of people today. When the Abu Sayyaf came across a Christian chapel in the jungle, they boasted, "There used to be a cross there, but we destroyed it. We hate the cross. Any time we see a cross we destroy it if we can."[10] The lives of Martin and Gracia spoke far louder than they understood during their captivity. They sowed seeds of grace and mercy, evident to their captors, that can be evaluated only in eternity. Never shall I forget ministering to men in the largest maximum-security prison in the Philippines when a prisoner approached me, gave me a hug, and then explained that he was one of the Abu Sayyaf terrorists who had taken the Burnhams captive. In broken English, he explained that he had become a captive of the Lord Jesus Christ and was following him.

Gracia Burnham learned more about herself during those darks days than she did about the Abu Sayyaf. Yet she discovered that God's grace is sufficient to survive without becoming destroyed by the hatred that drove her captors. She concludes her story by saying, "I resolve to keep living in the embrace of God's gladness and love for as long as he gives me breath." She learned what Paul knew—the triumph of the cross alone allows us to endure without losing heart.

---

[10] Ted Olson, "Did Martin die needlessly?" *Christianity Today,* vol. 47, no. 6 (2003): 35.

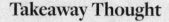

Takeaway Thought

Are you losing heart? Is discouragement slowly creeping into your soul, pushing away your faith and making you doubt that God loves you and that he is still in control? Gracia Burnham experienced this herself and God delivered her out of it. Hang on to God's promises and don't give up. Remember that God is seldom early, but he is never late.

MORE ABOUT HER STORY

In the Presence of My Enemies
by Gracia Burnham with Dean Merrill
(Tyndale House, 2010)

23

ELISABETH ELLIOT

Resting in God

On January 8, 1956, five young men intent on bringing the knowledge of Jesus Christ to the Huaorani people of Ecuador (then known as the Auca Indians) landed their little aircraft on a sandy strip of land adjacent to a jungle. Their mission, however, resulted in their deaths at the hands of a Huaorani tribe, leaving behind five widows, including Elisabeth Elliot, to grieve and try to cope with the great loss. Years later, I was doing a weekly television program and since Elisabeth Elliot's daughter Valerie and her son-in-law were friends living nearby, I asked her to extend an invitation to her mother to be a guest on my TV program.

The story of reaching the Huaorani was told at length by Elisabeth Elliot in her book *Through Gates of Splendor*. But when I asked her what kind of a person was her husband, Jim Elliot, she said, "He was never one to ask the question that many people ask today, 'Who am I?' but rather, 'Whose am I?' quoting 1 Corinthians 6:19, 'You are not your own; you were bought with a price. Therefore, honor God with your body.'"

After her husband Jim was martyred, Elisabeth took her daughter, then three years old, and went to live among the tribe who had killed her husband. During the three years she was there, she wrote to a friend, "I have now met four of the seven men who killed our husbands." Living in a leaf-thatched hut, eating roasted monkey limbs, and listening to frogs croaking at night, Elisabeth sought to translate the Bible into the Huaorani language. But her faith was challenged by difficult circumstances. Her translator was murdered, possibly because someone disliked his association with Elisabeth. A suitcase aboard a bus was either stolen or fell off the bus and three years of translation notes were lost. When her daughter Valerie asked if one of the tribesmen was her "daddy," Elisabeth knew it was time to return to the US to allow Valerie to become familiar with her family and start a new life.

Writing for *World Magazine*, Daniel Devine paid tribute to this remarkable woman, saying, "For the next half-century, Elliot made resting in God a life message. She was a best-selling author, speaker, professor, and radio host—teaching, encouraging readers and listeners to trust and obey a sovereign God, whatever the circumstances."[11] Her later years were both productive and challenging. She wrote twenty-eight books, one of her finest being

---

[11] Daniel James Devine, "Trust and Obey," *World Magazine*, vol. 30, no. 14 (July 11, 2015).

her biography of missionary Amy Carmichael, *A Chance to Die*.

After returning to the US, Elisabeth met and married a religion professor, Addison Leech, a prominent theologian and gracious encourager to Elisabeth. Their happiness, however, was cut short four years later as Addison died from cancer. Then one of her lodgers, Lars Gren, took a personal interest in Elisabeth, and when she learned of this she ordered him to leave her home; however, Lars was persistent and the two eventually married.

How did she respond to the losses and grief she experienced? She wrote, "God's ways are mysterious and our faith develops strong muscles as we negotiate the twists and turns of our lives." Another time, she said, "While it is perfectly true that some of my worst fears did, in fact, materialize, I see them now as 'an abyss and mass of mercies,' appointed and assigned by a loving and merciful Father who sees the end from the beginning. He asks us to trust Him."[12] And she did throughout her life.

---

[12] Devine, "Trust and Obey."

Takeaway Thought

God sustained Elisabeth Elliot through the years when she experienced grief and heartache at different stages of her life. Her example would enable millions to learn that deep peace is found in trusting God in all circumstances when one surrenders to his will and his great love. Elisabeth's faith remained strong and unwavering. She rested in God in all circumstances until he called her home. In the midst of chaos, from within and without, you, too, can find rest in God alone.

MORE ABOUT HER STORY

Through Gates of Splendor by Elisabeth Elliot
(Tyndale House, 1956)

24

AMY CARMICHAEL

A Humble Servant

Amy Carmichael was a woman who didn't fit the mold of what culture in the nineteenth century dictated a woman should be. Instead, she wanted to be molded by God's calling on her life. It is only proper that this selection should follow that of Elisabeth Elliot, in that Elliot's book, *A Chance to Die*, is the finest book in existence on the life of Amy Carmichael, one of the greatest missionaries in modern history.

Born on December 16, 1867, Amy grew up in a small village in Northern Ireland to devout Presbyterians, the oldest of seven children. One story of Amy's early life was her sadness that she had brown eyes rather than blue. She wished and hoped for her eyes to turn blue.

Having heard the Scottish missionary David Livingstone speak at a conference, Amy felt a call to serve God as a missionary in China and began preparation of serving in that capacity. Her health issues, however, made her realize that China was not where God actually wanted her to be. Floundering somewhat, she set sail for Japan, went briefly to China, and then traveled home. Arriving back in Ireland, she was entreated to just stay at home and serve God there. But listening to the prompting of the Holy Spirit instead of pressure from family and friends, she set sail for India, where she was to spend the rest of her life.

Upon arrival, Amy donned an Indian sari and darkened her skin with coffee—and her God-given brown eyes that she once wished were blue became one more thing that allowed her to better relate to the Indians she served. She insisted on being a humble servant. Amy became a thorn in the side of traditional missionaries who observed afternoon tea and never soiled their hands doing dirty work. In the early years of her work, there was a "Get Amy Carmichael out of India" movement among some missionaries and high-caste Indians.

Shortly after her arrival in India, she learned that a significant number of girls as well as little boys were being taken to the temple and forced into prostitution—allegedly being married to the gods—and then were made available to Hindu men. Amy would seize these children and take them home. On occasion, she would wade through a hostile crowd of shouting, angry people to rescue a little girl from temple prostitution and then weep openly with the child over the pain and hurt. More than once she faced trumped-up criminal charges of kidnapping. She was undeterred, convinced she was doing the will of God.

If the life of this woman who never was able to quite "fit the mold" of people's expectations could be captured in three words, these would be obedience, loyalty, and tenderness. Out of obedience to the will of God came absolute loyalty to those with whom she worked. She refused to speak against her critics and would not allow her coworkers to do so either. Amy was always self-depreciating. While serving in India, Amy received a letter from a young woman who was considering becoming a missionary. "What's missionary life like?" she asked, and Amy replied, "Missionary life is simply a chance to die!" That response became the title of Elisabeth Elliot's biography of her life.

In Amy's book, *Roots*, she wrote, "It is not at all that we think that ours is the only way of living, but we are sure that it is the way meant for us."

Eventually, Dohnavur Fellowship, the ministry Amy founded, became a mission that provided shelter and refuge for more than a thousand children. Amy's latter years were marred by a fall that left her paralyzed, and for much of the last twenty years of her life she was bedridden, but even then, she continued to write and to be an advocate for innocent children.

At the age of eighty-four, on January 18, 1951, Amy Carmichael slipped into the presence of the Lord. Under a tamarind tree, in a grave marked only by the Indian word for "mother," *Ammai,* lie the remains of a woman who was as much as a saint as anyone who ever lived.

Takeaway Thought

Was Amy Carmichael like a meteor that streaked across a darkened sky, having done something never to be repeated, or are there not others who are willing to give themselves without reservation to the call of God? Perhaps you are one of them!

MORE ABOUT HER STORY

A Chance to Die: The Life and Legacy of Amy Carmichael by Elisabeth Elliot (1987)

25

MAREN NEILSON

Forgiving but Never Forgetting

Among Maren Neilson's treasured possessions is a recipe book carefully written on sections of rough toilet paper bound by pieces of old string. What's so special about this unconventional recipe book and the woman who owns it?

Maren lived alone in a typical Norwegian cottage in the city of Tromso, near the Arctic Circle. Her brightly decorated house stood facing the fjord, and in the summer her garden was filled with beautiful flowers. Maren's sister, Reidun Gesswein, was a close friend of my wife and I, and it was through her that we were able to meet Maren and be welcomed into her home as she told us parts of the story of her life.

Her radiant smile and warm hospitality hardly reflected what she had been through. When World War II broke out, Maren had just married, and as all Norwegian patriots, her family wasn't happy when the Germans invaded Norway. Because Maren's husband and his family were active in the resistance movement, she was guilty by association and was arrested and sent to a concentration camp.

Perhaps you are unaware of the fact that the concentration camps of Hitler's Third Reich were not limited to Germany, or even Poland, but they were scattered across the face of Europe—several hundred of them—in every country the Nazis conquered. But no matter where they were located, they were operated with the same cruelty and the same dehumanization that considered people to be animals, less than human. Included on the list of victims of this cruelty were Maren Neilson and her husband.

Maren would have starved in the camp, but she had access to the garbage that came from the kitchen, so she would steal potato peelings in the night, hiding them until the matron who guarded her barracks was asleep. Then she would warm them on the tiny stove and share them with others. Unlike other camps, this one allowed visits from relatives once a month for no longer than five minutes, and during that time her visitors gave food to her. Whenever her family visited, they would bring the cakes and sweets that she missed. While they talked, Maren would literally stuff as much food into her mouth as she could eat before the guard came to cut the visit short.

But what about the recipe book written on toilet paper? All of the women who were starving were experienced cooks, and they would talk about their favorite recipes—cakes, cookies, shortbreads, reindeer roasts, and the other good things that they were denied in the concentration camp. For Maren's birthday, the older women put together a small recipe book of their favorites, something she will cherish to her dying day.

When the war ended and she and her husband were freed, Maren gradually picked up where her life had been interrupted, being active in her church, helping many who were in need, and serving wherever she could.

After hearing her tell her story, I asked, "Did you hate the Germans for what they did to you?" She replied, "No, I do not hate them, but we must not forget." She will never, ever forget. There are many variations on the phrase "We are doomed to repeat what we fail to remember," because it remains true.

God's grace brought healing and help to Maren, whose devout faith enabled her to keep hoping and trusting. "When you pass through the waters, I will be with you; and through the rivers, they shall not overwhelm you; when you walk through fire you shall not be burned, and the flame shall not consume you. For I am the LORD your God, the Holy One of Israel, your Savior" (Isaiah 43:2–3 ESV). This was the promise God gave to his people when they were in captivity. Thank God, it's still true for those such as Maren Neilsen who trust him and walk with him.

Takeaway Thought

Human nature tells you to hate those who persecute you. In Maren Neilson's case, she let go of hatred and chose to forgive instead. Hard to do, yes, but with God's help, it is possible. Forgive even if you might not be able to forget.

26

SVEA FLOOD

Her Remarkable Story of God's Sovereignty

In 1921, a missionary couple from Sweden named David and Svea Flood went with their two-year-old son David deep into Africa, to what was then called the Belgian Congo. There, they met another couple from Scandinavia who felt, like the Floods, that God was calling them to take the gospel from the main mission station to a more remote area. Though this was a giant leap of faith for them, they followed the Lord's leading and went to live just outside a village called N'dolera.

Though they prayed constantly for any sign of spiritual progress with the people, they saw little fruit. The only consistent contact they had with the village down the hill was through a young boy who sold them chickens and eggs twice a week. Svea, however, decided that even if he was the only African she could talk to, she would share the gospel with him. And after many weeks, the boy trusted Christ as his savior.

Later, Svea faced another challenge: she was pregnant, and far away from adequate medical facilities.

The village chief, who had been hostile to the Floods until this point, allowed a midwife to help her give birth. Svea gave birth to a little girl, whom she and her husband named Aina (pronounced A-ee-nah). However, the exhausting delivery on top of previous bouts of malaria severely weakened Svea. After seventeen days of prayer and struggle, she died. At first, the baby was given to the couple who had come to Africa with the Floods; but after they both passed away a few months later, she was adopted by an American couple who returned to the US. The baby's name was modified to Aggie.[13]

For Svea's husband David, it was the end of the "God trip." He turned his back on God, eventually remarried and had more children, but had one rule in the house: God was never to be spoken of. But God wasn't finished with him yet. Here's how the unbelievable chain of events unfolded.

Aggie grew up in the US and married Dewey Hurst, a pastor. One day she went to her mailbox and found a Swedish magazine. She couldn't read the words, but one picture caused her hands to perspire and her heart to race. It was a photo of a grave marked by a white cross, and on the cross was a name she did recognize: Svea Flood.

Aggie jumped in her car, drove to the office of a friend who could read Swedish and asked, "What does this

---

[13] For more about Aggie's story, see *Aggie: The Inspiring Story of a Girl Without a Country* by Aggie Hurst (Gospel Publishing House, 1986).

mean?" The story was about a missionary who had come to N'dolera, then part of the Belgian Congo in Africa. Because of the missionary, an African boy had grown up and built a school, leading the entire village to the Lord. It said that more than six hundred people had been converted.

After she read the article, she had a compulsion to go to Sweden and find her biological father. When she finally found his residence, she was surprised at what she saw. Walking into a filthy apartment strewn with liquor bottles, Aggie saw a broken man lying in a dirty bed. "Papa?" she said. And he turned to her, crying, "I never meant to give you away!"

"Papa," Aggie cried, "Jesus loves you. He has never hated you!" By the end of the afternoon, her father had come back to the God whom he had blamed for his wife's death many years before. Aggie told him the story she had learned in the magazine—that his wife, her mother, didn't die in vain, and that the little boy who sold them chickens and eggs grew up and became a powerful force for God, and that over six hundred people in the little village where they ministered were now Christians.

The story doesn't end there. Today, the man whom Svea led to Christ is the superintendent of the national church with well over 110,000 baptized believers. Svea Flood led only one small boy to Christ, but she left behind a legacy that impacted a nation!

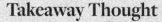

Takeaway Thought

Never hesitate to plant seeds of love and kindness. Learn from the experience of a relatively unknown woman named Svea Flood. Little did she know that her small act of obedience and faithfulness to God would someday produce such a great harvest of souls.

27

MARGARET BRAND

*Her Legacy of Love, Healing,
Faith, and Hope*

I missed meeting Drs. Paul and Margaret Brand by two weeks. My meeting with them was made impossible by Dr. Paul's serious illness, which eventually resulted in his promotion to heaven. When author Philip Yancey was preparing to spend time with the Brands before writing a book on their lives, his wife Janet told him, "The missing real story is Margaret Brand!" I agree.

Margaret left a legacy of love to her six children, twelve grandchildren, and two great-grandchildren and a legacy of healing to the thousands of people with leprosy whose eyesight she saved. She was an inspiration to the entire world as a humble woman who was self-effacing in the light of world renown as the number one authority on leprosy of the eye. She gave hope to thousands of people whose lives were forever changed by her example of servanthood.

Born in England to a doctor and his wife, Margaret always intended to follow in her father's footsteps. In

1937, she was one of the few women allowed into medical school. She finished at the top of her class, with Paul Brand, her future husband, in second. Speaking of their courtship, Margaret said, "I fell in love with him very quickly." Paul had grown up in India while Margaret had grown up in South Africa. Although Margaret's family were not Christians, both Paul and Margaret went to church together and felt that God would eventually use them in medical missions somewhere.

Margaret hoped it would be South Africa, but Paul was invited to join the Christian medical college in Vellore, India. At first, Margaret felt shrouded in a cloud of fear. As she prayed, though, the cloud of fear seems to dissipate, and she announced—over the strong objections of her parents and friends—"I'm going!" Margaret's training was in pediatrics, so imagine her surprise when the acting director of the hospital wrote to her—two weeks after Margaret had given birth to a baby—and said, "We don't wish to hurry you, but we must have more help in the eye department!"

Margaret thought, "She has to be joking!" Margaret had specifically told personnel she would work anywhere except in the eye department. She turned the paper over and wrote, "I don't mind being hurried, but I know nothing about eyes. You'll have to look for someone else. Sorry. Margaret." An hour later she got another message that said, "You'll learn. Please start on Monday."

She did, and in time she became the world's leading authority on the effects of leprosy on the eyes, lecturing and traveling all over the world. Why should so many people with leprosy have faltering eyes? Margaret had, in her own words, a burning curiosity to find out. She learned they lose sensitivity and feeling, and then rub the stubs of their hands into their eyes, introducing viruses to the cornea that eventually blind them.

Margaret could be persuasive when necessary. One leper who was losing his eyesight told another with the same affliction, "Better go to that lady doctor. She has a terrible temper."[14] Actually, she was a compassionate, gentle, caring woman who brought only healing and help to those who needed it. Philip Yancey observed, "She suffered with them." On one occasion she said, "I get the feeling God is much more involved in caring about suffering than you think." Her son-in-law, also a medical doctor, remarked that she had an "incarnational style of going down to the least of them and restoring the image of God.

The Brands moved to the US in 1966 and both served at the National Leprosarium in Carville, Louisiana for thirty-four years. Each brought a unique perspective and talent to bear on the needs of people.

For many years, I have kept a quote of Dr. Paul Brand's given in a lecture in 1990 titled, "The Wisdom of

---

[14] *The Story of Paul and Margaret Brand* (RBC Ministries, 2006), DVD.

the Body." He wrote, "I pray that when my time comes, I may not burble that my body has worn out too soon, but hold on to the gratitude that I have been so long at the help of the most wonderful creation the world has ever known and look forward to meeting the designer face to face."[15]

Both Margaret and her husband Paul are on the list of people whom I look forward to meeting when I cross into the presence of the Lord who long ago healed the sick with a word and a touch. Praise God who used both Margaret and Paul to bring healing and hope to thousands.

Takeaway Thought

God equips those he calls. Margaret Brand should know. God worked through her and brought healing to many people. What is hindering you from serving God—a fear of failure or sense of inadequacy? Take a step of courage today and start building your own legacy of faith.

MORE ABOUT HER STORY

Vision for God by Dr. Margaret Brand with Dr. James L. Jost (Discovery House, 2006)

---

[15] Paul Brand, "The Wisdom of the Body," *Chicago Sunday Evening Club*, Program 3428 (April 28, 1990).

28

KIM PHUC PHAN THI

The Napalm Girl

I f you ever saw her picture, you surely would remember it for the rest of your life. It gained fame in the 1970s as an anti-war icon when a photographer took her picture as she was running naked from a napalm bombing attack in Vietnam. The nine-year-old girl whose picture was so riveting became known as the "Napalm Girl," and the picture appeared in newspapers and magazines around the world.

As an adult, writing of the horrible and devastating event, Kim Phuc Phan Thi said, "I had not been targeted. I had simply been in the wrong place at the wrong time." Some forty-five years after that dark, hideous day, Kim has recorded the story of her life—the pain, the fear, the hatred, as well as the transformation that eventually purged the anger, bitterness, and resentment toward those who caused her suffering—in her book, *Fire Road*.

In a *Wall Street Journal* article featuring the book, she explains her transformation:

> My salvation experience occurred on Christmas Eve. It was 1982. I was attending a special worship service

at a small church in Vietnam. The pastor, Ho Hieu Ha, delivered a message many Christians would find familiar: Christmas is not about the gifts we carefully wrap and place under a tree. Rather it is about the gift of Jesus Christ, who was wrapped in human flesh and given to us by God. As the pastor spoke, I knew in my heart that something was shifting inside of me.

A decade removed from the defining tragedy of my life, I still desperately needed peace. I had so much hatred and bitterness in my heart. Yet I was ready for love and joy. I wanted to let go of my pain. I wanted to pursue life instead of holding fast to the front of the sanctuary to say 'yes' to Jesus Christ.[16]

As Kim grew in her faith, she realized that just as Jesus prayed on the cross—"Father, forgive them, for they know not what they do"—she also had to forgive those who were responsible for her suffering and give up, in her own words, the "crippling weight of anger, bitterness, and resentment."[17] For the rest of her life, she will require treatment for the burns that covered her arms, back, and neck, a constant reminder that we live in a broken world. If ever an individual has reason to hate those who caused her suffering, it would be Kim.

---

[16] Kim Phuc Phan Thi, "The Salvation of 'Napalm Girl," *The Wall Street Journal,* December 21, 2017.

[17] Kim Phuc Phan Thi, "The Salvation of 'Napalm Girl.'"

Writing to the Philippians, the apostle Paul counseled, "Be kind to each other, tenderhearted, forgiving one another, just as God through Christ has forgiven you" (Ephesians 4:32 NLT). Forgiveness is never easy when you have been deeply wronged. Our old natures cry out, "I want revenge!" It's been said that an eye for an eye and a tooth for a tooth leaves both people blind and toothless.

If you struggle with the issue of forgiveness, remember that forgiveness never means telling your offender, "What you did was okay"—because it was not okay. It simply means, "I give up my right to hurt you because you hurt me." It means you put anger, hatred, and revenge in the hands of God, who is very capable of righting the score. Never forget that even Jesus cried, "Father, forgive them, for they know not what they do" (Luke 23:34 ESV). If Kim could follow the example of Jesus and forgive, you can do the same thing.

Takeaway Thought

Kim Phuc Phan Thi personally experienced the devastation of war. Her body was scarred, but today her spirit has been made whole. God healed her heart, enabling her to be free from the pain, to let go of bitterness, and to offer forgiveness. Receive God's healing so you, too, can experience the liberating power of forgiveness.

MORE ABOUT HER STORY

Fire Road: The Napalm Girl's Journey through the Horrors of War to Faith, Forgiveness, and Peace by Kim Phuc Phan Thi (Tyndale House, 2017)

29

SHEILA LEECH

From the Gutter to God

Born in the late 1950s, Sheila Leech grew up in a small English village known as Bentley Heath. In her autobiography, she writes, "As I grew up, it became clear that I'd got the tomboy genes." She was baptized in a Catholic church as an infant, but after her dedicated Catholic grandmother passed away, her father began taking her and her siblings to a Brethren Sunday School.

Her Sunday school teacher prayed for Sheila, but at the same time she pled with God, "Please don't let Sheila Leech come to class today! Please keep her away!" God didn't answer that one. When Sheila got into a fight with another girl, she was told that there was only one person who could help her. "I know!" Sheila yelled, understanding that the Sunday school teacher was referring to Jesus Christ—but that's when Sheila turned her back on God and walked out of the church, not returning for many years.

Her life took a detour into everything that could distract her from God—alcohol, drugs, sex, and foul language. Then the Holy Spirit piqued her curiosity when she encountered Steve, an acquaintance who had been a hard drinker and drug user who got sober and, by his own testimony, became "committed to Jesus Christ." She knew he had something she longed for but didn't know how to find. Over the next couple of years, she occasionally went back to a Sunday evening gospel service and heard a version of the same message every time: "God loves you and will receive you if you will only come to him."

Then "something happened to me, something so strange, so unexpected, and so wonderful," she said. "I will never forget it." She met Jesus. But Sheila didn't experience instant change. She had a long way to go, and the next two years were spent in and out of a Christian rehabilitation facility to recover from substance abuse. Gradually, the Holy Spirit, whom Sheila depended on to guide her life, became real to her.

Then friends told her about the need for someone in Ecuador to provide assistance for an elderly couple. But she could think of no reasons why this should be of concern to her. After all, she didn't feel "called" (whatever that meant). She didn't know Spanish or the indigenous language spoken where the couple were living, and—bottom line—she had no money! Good reasons to stay home and forget Ecuador, right? Dead wrong. Things came together and Sheila was off on the adventure of her life.

In her book, *God Knows What I'm Doing Here*, Sheila tells the story of her years serving in difficult to impossible situations as a nurse, caring both for people's physical and spiritual needs. She survived numerous brushes with near death and disaster—not only in Ecuador but in Pakistan and Lebanon, going where there was no one else to help. Sheila stopped asking why and began to say, "Why not?" She endured privation, and at times suffering, working with insufficient resources but always praying, asking for the grace of God and enough strength to minister to just one more person.

What the story of this misfit, rowdy youth demonstrates is that no one is beyond the love and grace of God. If you dare to follow the still but powerful voice of the Holy Spirit, you will not have tested the resources of God until you have attempted the impossible.

As Sheila has often said, "Why not?" She would embark on exciting adventures that became a testimony to God's protection, power, and persistence. At times, her heart would cry out, "I don't know what I'm doing here but God knows what I'm doing here."

Takeaway Thought

Do you ever look at a person and say, 'They will never be a Christian'? Take it from Sheila Leech, who made a 180-degree turn and is now serving God in challenging places. Good thing that God doesn't disqualify anybody from being saved. That's what grace is all about.

MORE ABOUT HER STORY

God Knows What I'm Doing Here
by Sheila V. Leech (Authentic Media, 2017)

30

GRACE AGAR

The Bookseller Turned Missionary

In retirement, Grace Agar filled notebooks with handwritten quotes and resource materials and gave them to pastors. If she heard a series of Bible teachings that she liked, she would take copious notes in composition notebooks and later make handwritten copies to share with others. When one of those notebooks fell into my hands, I looked at the carefully scripted pages and thought, "What an unusual woman who would take the time to prepare these!" Little did I know that the woman who spent hours crafting these notebooks was a dedicated, focused woman who wasn't afraid of much of anything.

Born in 1877, Grace was walking to high school in San Francisco, California one morning, when she felt that God was saying, "The foreign mission field!" Three mornings in a row, she felt that urgency, and like the prophet Samuel when he was a child, Grace said, "Yes, Lord!" That commitment prompted her to take the first step toward a life of ministry in China.

A scholarship led her to Mills College, a rather exclusive women's college which gave her a sound liberal arts education but little by way of a knowledge of Scripture. She later wrote, "During my last term I felt strongly that I must go to Bible school, but it was virtually impossible for my parents to send me."[18] She had five siblings and her family did not have enough money to go around. Grace could count on no help from her parents.

One day, she picked up a Christian magazine which said, "Anyone who sells five thousand Moody Colportage books in eight months may have a scholarship of ten months at the Moody Bible School." That was it. Grace knew what she had to do. With fifty dollars of borrowed money, she ordered the first five hundred of the little books. With more tenacity than a car salesman, Grace approached friends and acquaintances alike. To her, everybody was a potential buyer. She sold a thousand books, then two, then three. Finally, she was down to the last five hundred as the clock was ticking.

Of this experience, she later wrote, "On the last day of the allowed eight months I still had five hundred books to sell. I rushed to the Post Office to place my order and it was closed!" Inside she could see a postal attendant. Not to be defeated, she went to the back door of the post office and knocked. The postal clerk, taking pity on this

---

[18] Quotes in this story are from the biography of Grace Agar in *The Holy Spirit and Mission Dynamics,* ed. C. Douglas McConnell (William Carey Library, 1997).

girl who poured out her story, agreed to come back after supper and help her.

As she left the post office after purchasing the money order which would put her over five thousand books sold, a Salvation Army band nearby began playing an old song called "Hallelujah, 'Tis Done."

In 1902, after studying at Moody Bible School, Grace boarded a ship for China. Her friends said, "You are crazy to go now!" They had a point. Only months before, the Boxer rebellion in China had taken the lives of hundreds of missionaries and foreigners. Undaunted, she sailed alone for China, where she ministered for twenty-eight years. Grace had no formal medical training, but she was willing to do what needed to be done when someone was suffering. She alleviated the misery of many by pulling diseased teeth when there was no dentist around and people begged for her help.

One of her newsletters read as follows:

Yesterday an old man accepted the Lord so gladly, and in the evening six soldiers were converted. Some of our Christians brought a whole small village to Christ, where four brothers and their wives with their 17 children have destroyed their idols, burning their very old ancestral tablets which they have venerated for many years, and have posted Christian posters on their walls. This is truly a work of the living God. It was touching to see a tribesman with tears in his eyes and joy in his face accepting Christ. He said so humbly, "I am so stupid, but I want to believe in the true God."

Forced to leave the field of her calling when civil war erupted in China in 1937, she eventually retired, but she never relented in her service for the Lord, painstakingly filling notebook after notebook with resource materials for pastors and Christian workers. Those handwritten notebooks in my library with pages that are now turning yellow with age are treasures, a heritage from a tough lady who never quit or gave up. May God raise up more people with the kind of stuff Grace Agar was made of!

Takeaway Thought

Nothing stopped Grace Agar from achieving her goal. She was persistent in selling books, working as a missionary overseas, and serving God in her unique way in her retirement. May you be inspired by this woman who never knew what it meant to give up.

31

MAVIS ORTON

Midwife to the Poor

When God decides to change the course of human history, he doesn't always send an army. Sometimes he sends a baby—a tiny, helpless bundle weighing but a few pounds.

On November 26, 1932, a baby girl was born in Tamworth, England and was christened Mavis Orton. As a teenager, Mavis attended a Methodist missionary rally and felt God speaking to her about becoming a missionary nurse, but she couldn't picture herself as a nurse. Instead, she joined the Red Cross and worked as a volunteer in a hospital on weekends. God's call, however, could not be silenced, and at the age of twenty-six, she entered nursing school. Upon graduation, she worked as a nurse in Sutton, Coldfield, England.

In 1966, her heart was touched by the needs of people in developing countries. She agreed to go to Thailand to provide needed medical assistance. Her aging mother, however, had a stroke and Mavis decided she was needed at home where she could take care of her mother. Her plans for serving abroad were put aside for twenty years.

After her mother passed away, Mavis began making contacts with mission organizations. But when they learned her age, they said, "Thanks but no thanks! You are much too old." Then Mavis heard of Action International, headed by Doug Nichols, who liked her "can do" spirit and invited her to work with them in the Philippines.

Mavis arrived in Manila and began to learn Tagalog, the language spoken there. She went to work in Antipolo, a rather poor area outside Manila. Learning that the area had one of the highest infant mortality rates in the Philippines, Mavis decided to do something about it. She rented a two-bedroom house and converted one of the bedrooms into a birthing center. Mavis said, "People simply couldn't afford to pay midwives or go to a hospital. Many young mothers said, 'Giving birth is like having one foot in the grave!'"[19] She thought, "Why shouldn't these women and babies be getting the care they need?" So Mavis brought the expectant mothers into her tiny home, helping them give birth in a safe and dignified manner. The little house turned into the Shalom Christian Birthing Home where, for the next three decades, Mavis worked with poor women and trained midwives while delivering literally hundreds of babies.

People began to recognize the contribution of this determined woman who was making a difference in the

---

[19] Author interview.

lives of many Filipinas. Writing an article for *Readers Digest* titled, "Special Deliveries," Sarah Etchells began, "The midwife, a 77-year-old nurse named Mavis Orton, holds up a baby—a beautiful little girl. 'I'm happy to hear the sound of a newborn's cry,' she says. The baby's mother smiles, rolls over and closes her eyes. She is exhausted. Amazingly, after six hours, she will get up from her thin mattress, walk out of the house with her baby, get into a trike (a motorcycle with a sidecar) and head off."[20]

Even Queen Elizabeth noticed and gave tribute to this servant of the Lord. On June 13, 2007, Her Majesty Queen Elizabeth II bestowed on Mavis the Member of the Most Excellent Order of the British Empire (MBE) at Buckingham Palace in London.

Asked if she was honored to receive the MBE as an acknowledgment of her work, Mavis deflected the praise by saying, "I do think the award is an excellent opportunity given by God to share the needs of the ministry in the Philippines, a country of over 90 million people." She then mentioned her plan to find the funds for a multi-story facility that eventually was built and allowed hundreds of women to deliver healthy babies, whether or not they could pay for the services they received.

Thank God for the potential that every newborn has. No wonder Jesus said, "Let the little children to come to

---

[20] Sarah Etchells, "Special Deliveries," *Reader's Digest Asia* (July 2010).

Me, and do not forbid them; for of such is the kingdom of heaven" (Matthew 19:14 NKJV).

Takeaway Thought

Has anybody ever told you that you're too old, too weak, or too ignorant to do something big for God? Mavis Orton didn't let her age keep her from pursuing her mission. As long as you are totally committed to love God and people, you can pursue any calling that God puts in your heart.

32

NADIA PACHENKO

The Chernobyl Doctor

The email was shocking. Though I knew her frail body was fighting cancer, I wasn't prepared for the bluntness of the message which read, "Nadia is dead. She died at 1:10 AM this morning." The sender was Nadia's daughter, Ania.

I first met Professor Dr. Nadia Pachenko in 1996, and was immediately drawn to this no-nonsense woman who stood about five feet in stature but was a giant among those who loved children and ministered to their needs whether or not there was money to pay for their care.

In the early hours of the morning on April 25, 1986, a nuclear reactor at Chernobyl exploded in an orange ball of flame. Located some eighty miles north of Kyiv, Ukraine, the four Chernobyl nuclear reactors produced most of the electricity in Ukraine, then part of the USSR. A chain reaction produced an out-of-control inferno that blew the heavy steel and concrete lid from reactor number four. Thirty people were immediately killed. People living in the nearby town of Prijat knew something had gone wrong, but no one imagined how devastating and horrendous

it actually was. For seventy-two hours, people were told nothing but to stay indoors. Then they were told to take personal belongings for about a three-day evacuation. They never returned.

When I visited Chernobyl several years after the disaster, we boarded a government bus wearing protective clothing. The officer in charge periodically checked a Geiger counter, which registered the increased radiation as we approached the reactor, then covered by a vast sarcophagus of concrete. When the Geiger counter stopped working, he thumped it, muttering about the poor workmanship of the Soviet instruments they worked with.

What did we find? It was like a twilight zone. Clothes were still on the lines. Looking in the window of a school nearby, we saw books and papers scattered on the floor. A rusted Ferris wheel in the nearby village stood silent. Vivid in my memory was the sight of desolation caused by the radioactive wind blowing north towards Belarus and the Scandinavian countries. The landscape was black and lifeless, like a giant knife had slashed the forest.

Dr. Nadia Pachenko had been the chief medical officer for Chernobyl, coordinating efforts to treat people and minister to their needs. She told me that regardless of the level of radiation, she and the other doctors were instructed to write down the minimal levels so the government could attest that nothing out of the ordinary had taken place.

When government funding for care ran out, Dr. Pachenko opened her own clinic, and that's when I was first introduced to this dedicated servant and compassionate woman who continued to evaluate, test, and treat people, especially children.

Despite what the government-controlled media said, Dr. Pachenko believed that at least 80 percent of the children in Ukraine were adversely affected by the Chernobyl explosion. Water that cooled the giant nuclear reactors came from the Dnieper River and flowed to Kyiv, where it became drinking water. But this is not a story about the problem; it's about a woman who was a hero who continued her work in spite of no funding, little equipment, and no official recognition.

Shortly before her homegoing she wrote the following to me:

> I was born in a family of unbelievers and nobody ever told me about God. When I was a student at the University, we had to study atheism and origins of life according to Darwin. Only when I began working independently I discovered the mystery of creation. I studied the blood cells. The more I studied them, the more I thought about them. The blood cell "witnessed" to me about the Creator. That is how I came to Christ.

Dr. Pachenko succumbed to cancer, as have countless others who were exposed to the effect of the worst nuclear disaster in history. But she will long be remembered for her labor of love, her tireless effort to make a difference, and her determination to do what she could.

The Gospels tell a story of a woman who brought an alabaster jar filled with precious perfume and poured it on the feet of Jesus in an act of worship. The disciples rebuked her, but Jesus affirmed her saying, "She has done what she could!" And I am certain that he would have said the same for this noble woman—Nadia Pachenko.

Takeaway Thought

Dr. Nadia Pachenko, in her crusade to protect and preserve the health of the people following the Chernobyl disaster, didn't think twice about laying her own well-being on the line. She became their champion who ultimately had to pay a high price. Are you just as willing to take big risks and sacrifice?

33

EDITH SCHAEFFER

Beautiful Happiness

Edith Schaeffer died at the age of ninety-eight in Gryon, Switzerland, a beautiful mountain-studded country she had grown to love and claim as her own. She was the third daughter of a couple who ran a school for girls and served as missionaries. From her birth in Wenzhou, China to the work she has chosen to do, Edith never quite fit the "cookie cutter" mold of women of her generation.

On June 25, 1932, seventeen-year-old Edith attended a church service in a liberal Presbyterian church where a Unitarian minister delivered an address on "How I know that Jesus is not the Son of God, and how I know that the Bible is not the Word of God." As she was gathering her thoughts to rebut the speaker, a young man stood to his feet and announced, "My name is Francis Schaeffer and I want to say that I know Jesus is the Son of God, and he is also my Savior." Little did she know that the same young man was to become her husband and life partner.[21]

---

[21] Joe Carter, "9 Things You Should Know About Edith Schaeffer," *The Gospel Coalition* (April 1, 2013).

"To put her husband through three years of seminary, Edith tailored men's suits and made ballroom gowns and wedding dresses. From cow skin she made belts sold in New York stores."[22] After three years of ministry in the US, the Schaeffers moved their family to Switzerland to assist churches as well as to meet disbelief and liberalism head-on, providing a shelter for those with searching hearts and an answer for those with an open mind. Their work eventually came to be known as L'Abri, a French word meaning "shelter." Eventually their work gained international recognition as TIME magazine did a feature on their ministry. Edith was a multi-talented woman who painted, served as a hostess, impacted many lives on a one-to-one basis, and used her skills to write twenty books, two of which won Gold Medallion Awards: Affliction and The Tapestry. Her 1975 book, *What Is a Family?*, did not shy away from controversies of her day. In this book, she wrote, "There needs to be a homemaker exercising some measure of skill, imagination, creativity, desire to fulfill needs and give pleasure to others in the family. How precious a thing is the human family. Is it not worth some sacrifice in time, energy, safety, discomfort, and work? Does anything come forth without work?"

---

[22] Udo Middelmann, "A Work of Art," *World Magazine* (April 20, 2013).

She lived the life she wrote about. Her Sunday evening "High Teas" attracted as many as fifty guests to her home each Sunday evening to share tea and a meal, all paid for with royalties from her books. Guests at L'Abri found flowers, twigs from local trees, and moss decorating their tables. Edith began a newsletter for women known as "Family Letters" that grew in popularity to a circulation of over 13,000.

Edith found enjoyment in people, regardless of their persuasion, beliefs, and background. She accepted them as they were, where they were—in the market, on a plane, or on a street corner. When she was born in China, her parents gave her a Chinese name, Mei Fuh, meaning "Beautiful happiness." She lived up to it. That she brought happiness to a vast number of people is to describe the purpose of her life.

In a real sense, the life of Edith Schaeffer was lived as a beautiful tapestry which was as fresh and crisp as the air on a Swiss mountaintop and as unusual as finding a diamond in a garden.

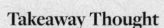

Takeaway Thought

Do you have the gift of spreading happiness? If you think you don't, ask the Holy Spirit to work in your heart so you can find joy in making others happy. Edith Schaeffer found fulfillment in the many things—big or small—that she did for people.

MORE ABOUT HER STORY

"A Work of Art" by Udo Middelmann
in *World Magazine* (April 20, 2013)

34

ROSA PARKS

A Woman with Quiet Strength

It is extremely doubtful that Rosa Parks awakened on Thursday December 1, 1955 suspecting that on that day she would be going to jail, or that her profile would be in every newspaper and her story featured on every TV program for several days.

Growing up as an African American, Rosa felt the bitter taste of racial discrimination, especially in Alabama. She had seen the Ku Klux Klan march past her house while her father stood outside with a shotgun, prepared to use it if his home was desecrated.

Rosa was a devout Christian who regularly attended and participated in the life of the African Methodist Episcopal Church. In her book, *Quiet Strength*, she wrote, "Daily devotions played an important part in my childhood. Every day before supper and before we went to services on Sundays, my grandmother would read the Bible to me, and my grandfather would pray. I remember finding such comfort and peace while reading the Bible; its teachings became a way of life and helped me in dealing with day-to-day problems."[23] As her knowledge of the Bible increased, she became convinced that "the Bible had a social mandate in its message, too, one that taught Rosa that people should stand up for rights, just as the children of Israel stood up to the Pharaoh."[24]

When push came to shove, it was Rosa Parks who refused to stand up to give her seat to a white man. She had spent the day working at the Montgomery Fair Department Store, and at the end of the day she boarded a bus, paid her fare, and sat down in an empty seat in the first row of seats that were reserved for blacks. As more passengers boarded the bus, several white men were forced to stand in the aisles. Then the bus driver demanded that four black passengers give up their seats for the white men. Three did. One did not—Rosa Parks! As Eric Metaxas wrote in his book *7 Women and the Secret of Their Greatness*, "The tired seamstress and the bus driver, James Blake, were about to make history." Blake asked her, "Why don't you stand up?" She responded, "I don't think I should have to stand up!" The driver then called the police. Two officers boarded the bus and escorted her to city hall where the police headquarters was located. At city hall, Rosa asked to get a drink at a nearby water fountain. One office told her

[23] Rosa Parks, *Quiet Strength: The Faith, the Hope, and the Heart of a Woman Who Changed a Nation* (Zondervan, 1994), 54.

[24] Rosa Parks as quoted by Eric Metaxas in *7 Women and the Secret of Their Greatness* (Thomas Nelson, 2015), 140.

to go ahead and get a drink while another one intervened, shouting, "You can't drink no water. It's for whites only. You have to wait till you get to the jail."

If ever there was an unlikely candidate to become a national icon and help to radically change the mindsets of millions of people, it was Rosa Parks. She had her day in court and was fined ten dollars, plus four dollars in court costs. Rosa appealed her conviction and challenged the legality of discrimination, inspiring many to join a movement to battle the virus of racial discrimination.

For the rest of her life, she remained active in the civil rights movement, particularly in politics, education, and fair housing. She was called the American "First Lady of Civil Rights" and selected to be one of the people to meet Nelson Mandela on his release from prison. She was awarded the Presidential Medal of Freedom by President Bill Clinton and the Congressional Gold Medal, the highest award of the US Congress.

Takeaway Thought

Are you or is someone you know a victim of discrimination? What can you do to rise above it? Rosa Parks refused to be bullied to submission and stood up for her rights and the rights of others. God loves all of us unconditionally. Don't let anybody convince you that you are worth any less.

MORE ABOUT HER STORY

7 Women and the Secret of Their Greatness
by Eric Metaxas (Thomas Nelson, 2015)

35

JACQUIE CHEVALIER

Balance in Beauty

In the late 1970s, Jacquie Chevalier was a long way from New York, the city of her birth, where as a child, she had designed and made clothes for her dolls. Now living in Manila, Philippines with her husband, she had long ago left behind her life as a model who loved to wear stylish and trendy clothes. As a young woman, Jacquie had attended the Barbizon School of Modeling. She describes her ethnicity by saying, "I'm part American Indian (Cherokee), French, Creole, African-American, and English."[25] Jacquie's godly mother was a powerful influence in her life and encouraged her to be anything God wanted her to be. Her father, a retired staff sergeant, served in World War II under General George Patton and was a personal friend of Jackie Robinson, who was credited with breaking the color barrier in baseball.

At age twenty-six, she attended a Christian rock concert and heard a clear presentation of the gospel, yielding her heart to the Lord who changed her life. At the

---

[25] Quotes in this story are from an author interview (June 2016).

same time, a young man, Wil Chevalier, who was climbing the corporate ladder to success, won her heart. They eventually got married. It was shortly after that I began spending time with Wil, encouraging and discipling him. Sensing that both were highly committed to God's purpose, I challenged them to consider going to the Philippines and taking over working with my ministry there.

One of their goals in the Philippines was to disciple twelve couples, who in turn could disciple others. First, Wil and Jacquie led those who helped in their home to the Lord—a house helper and a driver. Then, Jacquie was invited to cohost a Christian TV program for women. Around that time, Helen Cadd (whose story is also told in this book) challenged Jacquie to use her skills, including modeling, designing clothes, and cosmetology, to reach successful and wealthy women in the Philippines. God had been speaking to Jacquie about developing a seminar known as "Balance in Beauty," where she would help women learn colors, styles, and to wear clothes that enhanced their skin tone, hair, and eye colors. In short, Jacquie gave a crash course for women on how to "put their best foot forward."

In Asia, Jacquie discovered that (like in many cultures) social classes observe unwritten distinctions and are not mixed—something that is foreign to God's love and concern. In the Philippines, with its strict cultural class distinctions, naysayers told her that it would be impossible in Filipino culture to conduct seminars which "mixed the poor with the rich." They warned that the Bible study groups that had been formed through contacts with women who responded to her seminars should be separate. And how did Jacquie respond? "We felt strongly that God would use his Word to work in and through everyone involved, so we went ahead with the studies, mixing people on all levels of society as well as Chinese, Filipino, American, and other nationalities."

Jacquie's gracious disposition was disarming. Because she cared for everyone, those who were impacted by her life began to use their own resources and influence to make a difference in the lives of those who were disenfranchised by a culture that often failed to recognize the inner beauty that comes as Christ indwells and empowers a life. Jacquie says, "The only way to become truly beautiful on the outside is to have beauty on the inside, one that loves people regardless of their class or financial status."

She has done Balance in Beauty seminars with owners of major corporations and government officials as well as for those who live in neglected areas, giving encouragement, love, and help to all, breaking barriers and class distinctions.

In her gracious, gentle, and loving manner, Jacquie has followed Jesus' pattern—reaching out to all women, showing them his love, and helping them understand that real beauty begins as Jesus takes up residence within a heart, and that radiance enhances the natural beauty without.

A postscript you need to know: The original twelve couples whom Wil and Jacquie sought to disciple have, in turn, discipled a large group of others who, in turn, have reached even more, fulfilling Jesus' command to "go make disciples!" (Matthew 28:19). What a wonderful way to serve God. Jacquie has used a unique skill set to help fulfill the Great Commission!

Takeaway Thought

Do you sometimes feel that you are not gifted? Are you envious of those who stand on stage and are able to deliver powerful messages, earning the admiration of the crowd? Just like Jacquie Chevalier, maybe you have a unique skill set that you can share to help others. There are things you can do that nobody else can. Give everything you have to the Lord.

36

NOAH'S WIFE

The Mother of Everyone You Will Ever Meet

You can trace your lineage to this woman, yet history does not actually give us her name. How can someone so important be so ignored? Today, all the people in the world—regardless of their heritage—are descended from her. But we know next to nothing about her background and the details of her life, including where she was born, where she lived, how she met her husband, and where she was buried. We do know that she lived during a period of great calamity and distress, unlike anything that the world has ever known before or even since she walked on earth. We do know, too, that she supported her husband and became a woman who rightfully took her place in the annals of history.

Who was she? No, not Eve, the first woman to have been created. Though her story is also told in the book of Genesis in the Bible, this woman was at least ten generations removed from Mother Eve. Moses, who wrote Genesis, simply identifies her as the wife of Noah, the one who built an ark to escape the devastation of the world's Great Flood (Genesis 7:7).

For someone who was so important to all humanity, so very little has been written about her. Her husband is mentioned over fifty times in the Bible. For instance, Moses said that Noah was "a righteous man, blameless among the people of his time, and he walked faithfully with God" (Genesis 6:9). Ezekiel, who was born hundreds of years after the flood, described Noah as being a man of righteousness (Ezekiel 14:14). In the New Testament, Peter—the one who walked on water, the boisterous one who seemed to always have an opinion about almost everything—made mention of Noah in both of his books. What did Peter say about Noah? That he was "a preacher of righteousness" (2 Peter 2:5; see also 1 Peter 3:20).

Noah's wife was a woman whose true worth has never been articulated, nor has due credit been given to her. To better understand her importance, I will direct your attention to three snapshots that shed light on her character and person.

Snapshot one is the wife of a very unpopular preacher. As the saying goes, behind every successful man is a woman—a mother, a wife, or, perhaps, a teacher. How challenging it must've been to live with a man who was the mockery of his day—a man building a giant boat for a coming catastrophic flood everyone thought was impossible!

Snapshot two is the mother of three sons who grew up playing with the children of those whose values were vastly different from what she and her husband held. The Bible says that "the earth was corrupt in God's sight and was full of violence," but Noah "walked faithfully with God" (Genesis 6:6, 9). Surely she had to wipe tears from her boys' eyes when their friends mocked them because of the strange ideas of their father. Yet not one of her sons was lost. Think how she would have answered the questions of her sons who asked, "Why can't I? Everybody else is doing it!"

Snapshot three is the grandmother who lived through one of the biggest events in history. While it is uncertain how many grandchildren she actually had, think of the tales she must have told when an innocent-eyed grandchild said, "Grandmother, tell us a story." What vivid eyewitness accounts of the flood those grandchildren must have heard!

Surely Noah's wife could be included with the heroes of whom the author of Hebrews wrote, "The world was not worthy of them" (Hebrews 11:38).

Takeaway Thought

Noah's wife never got the recognition that she deserved for, among other things, helping Noah take care of an ark full of people and animals. But she was there alongside Noah every step of the way. When God asks you to do something for him, are you willing to do it even if it means going against popular opinion and enduring the ridicule of people who don't know God?

MORE ABOUT HER STORY

Genesis 6:9–8:22

37

MARJAANA SEILONEN

No Ordinary Woman

Growing up in her native Finland, Marjaana Seilonen came to faith in her Lord Jesus Christ, and dreamed of someday being a missionary in Africa. As an adult in the 1990s, Marjaana moved to Southern California and began attending Saddleback Community Church. It was there that she heard Sister Freda (whose story is also in this book) talk about the needs of Kenya, and her heart was warmed. When Sister Freda urged others to come to Africa, Marjaana immediately said, "Yes, I'm going. I'm going!" She was the first to sign up with a group that was to visit Sister Freda's work. (To date, she has made the trip twenty-three times.)

Upon arrival in Kitale, Kenya, the team of men and women in the group were organized in smaller groups to visit a variety of churches. Marjaana's group was taken to visit a small congregation who met in a metal shack at the back of the market in Kiminini. The church had a packed dirt floor and the people were extremely poor. They sang, however, with a sincerity and earnestness that was lacking, she thought, in American churches.

Marjaana sensed the empowering of the Spirit of God when the pastor, Shadrack Barasa, spoke. Pastor Shadrack saw needs and strove to meet those needs as he could. He recognized that basic skills that would make the people employable were needed. First, he started to teach automobile mechanics to young men. Then he added carpentry. He and his wife also attempted to start a training program teaching young women to sew. The demand, however, overwhelmed their capacity to meet it. When they announced that they were offering a basic sewing class, some two hundred people wanted to take it. The problem? There were only two sewing machines.

When Marjaana saw the needs in Kenya, she felt convicted. She spoke of Pastor Shadrack, saying, "He was doing so much with so little." Returning to her home in Southern California, she asked herself, "What am I doing with the resources I have?" What she had seen—poverty, suffering, inadequate medical resources, and the faces of hungry children—stayed on her mind. "I've got to return," she thought. Making contact with Pastor Shadrack, she asked, "What could we do?" His response was, "Why don't you bring a medical team with you and do a clinic?" Then he added that he would be grateful for her to also hold a women's conference at his church.

Marjaana had no medical experience, but she had a simple faith and a conviction that God would supply the needs if he wanted her to return. She set a goal of an amount of money so large that if the money was given, she would know God wanted her to go back. Within a few weeks she had raised $10,000 for medical needs and $4,000 for women's ministries, and her garage was overflowing with medical supplies that had been donated. In 2004, She understood that God wanted her to go back to Kenya and take a group of friends with her.

When she returned, more than three thousand people were treated at the two-day clinic, and, following a presentation of the *JESUS* film, over one hundred people trusted in the Lord Jesus Christ. This was the start of a unique ministry known as Outreach to the World, spearheaded by Marjaana and a few friends who were committed to making a difference in the lives of needy people.

Marjaana's ministry wisely addresses needs, then allows Kenyans to assume responsibility for them. Helping to provide clean water, education, getting children off the streets where they sniff glue and steal, and finding adults employment, especially for young women, are the priorities. Marjaana finds homes for the homeless where their needs are met, and they are not abused. Instead of warehousing orphans, she strives to place an orphaned child with family (usually a relative, often a grandmother). As I'm writing this, the ministry's most recent newsletter is filled with pictures and names of young women who are enrolling in college or the School of Nursing, learning skills that will allow them to be self-sustaining and independent.

Never doubt that a small group of committed Christians can make a big difference in the lives of many. Marjaana Seilonen has demonstrated that!

Takeaway Thought

How easy it is to forget sometimes that there are people in some parts of the world who do not have access to basic services. Marjaana Seilonen saw the need and did something to meet it. If God stirs your heart to move, follow his lead.

MORE ABOUT HER STORY

Heart of Compassion, Hands of Care
by Darlene Sala (Wingspread Publishers, 2008)

38

HELEN CADD

The Inconvenient Adventurer

G. K. Chesterton once said, "An adventure is an inconvenience rightly considered." If so, Helen Cadd sure had a lot of "inconvenient adventures"—the kinds she would go on to write about in a book by the same name.

In 1949, Helen met her husband Dick at Pacific College, a Christian college in Oregon (now known as George Fox University). As a teenager, Helen used to say that the person she married could not be short, nor could he have red hair. She changed her mind, however, when she met Dick. He was both! Being musically gifted, Dick needed an accompanist to travel with him. Although she didn't consider it her primary gift, Helen developed her piano-playing skills to assist him. In fact, Helen would become such a skilled musician that later she went on to play the trumpet and perform for many famous people, including US President Ronald Reagan and Philippine President Cory Aquino.

While hospitality might not technically be included in the apostle Paul's list of spiritual gifts, it's still certainly a gift from God—and Helen had that gift in abundance. Her tender heart resulted in her touching the lives of hungry, often neglected people. Whenever she saw a needy person by the side of the road, Helen would always have something in her car that she could give to them. There were many months when she fed fifty or more people— guests whom she invited to join her family for a meal and fellowship. At Christmas, she spearheaded an annual drive to provide tubs of food, medicine, and resources for people in need, accompanied by singing, games, and the Christmas story.

Dick and Helen have five children, all of them uniquely talented, who adopted the same values as their parents. One became a teacher. Another a nurse. One is a missionary pilot, and another a film producer whose ministry is not only to film stories in Asia that need to be told, but to equip local groups to do the work and then leave the video equipment behind for them to be self-sustaining. The fifth travels the world as a photographer.

As a friend, I have observed that Helen has the convictions that she has conveyed to her children. First and foremost, attitude is everything. While you have no choice in what happens to you, you do have a choice as to how you respond to it. All of the Cadd children have encountered many situations in life that required resiliency when "life happened." One of these situations was the time the Cadds were aboard a ship on their way to the Philippines when they were advised that they would have to leave the ship in Hawaii and make other arrangements to get to Hong Kong, where they would get Philippine visas. They arrived in Hong Kong, with thirty-three pieces of luggage and five very weary children. But instead of being miffed over the Hong Kong detour, Helen convinced the family that this was a wonderful opportunity to sightsee and learn about a new culture.

"Attitude check!" was the cry that rang through the Cadd house when things were going sour. Their mother reminded her children that you grow either bitter or better when unexpected things happen. Helen herself demonstrated that the day she arrived home in suburban Manila and saw (in her words), "Little Filipino boys of assorted ages and sizes were running in and out of my house! Some were carrying glasses of juice and eating cookies. They were noisy, excited and dirty, but obviously having a good time." Then her son Jon (now a missionary pilot in Africa) said, "These are my new friends. Fellows, meet my mom. She's the greatest!"

Helen believed that no matter what happened, God would take them through it. When the family was touring the Netherlands, their daughter Yvonne was struck by a car which resulted in life-threatening injuries. The story of how God provided the care Yvonne needed to recover, even to being airlifted to the US, taking nine seats on a jet, was one illustration of his care.

Helen lives out her belief that nothing is impossible with God. Repeatedly, her prayers have been answered in such a manner that everyone knew it could not have just happened. It had to be God who opened or closed doors. Her children grew up holding on to this lesson in faith and are living it out themselves.

Now retired, Helen continues to graciously extend hospitality—opening her home to those in need, her prayers for those who hurt, and her love for everyone she meets. What a wonderful example of God's care!

Takeaway Thought

God gave Helen Cadd a love for people and the gift of hospitality. Always positive in her attitude, she believes that God can and will take her through difficult circumstances. Adopt the same attitude as hers and soon you will realize that life is better lived this way.

MORE ABOUT HER STORY

Inconvenient Adventures by Helen Cadd
(Xulon Press, 2016)

39

GRACIELA LACEY

A Beautiful Life

The life of Graciela Lacey is a beautiful testimony of how the unrelenting grace of God changed her from being (in her own words) "an ugly-hearted woman hating everyone and everything in life—depressed, miserable, sad, empty, lonely, and rejecting Christ to a cheerful, smiling woman."[26]

Graciela was born in Mexico, one of fourteen children. When she was ten years old, her father died. With so many mouths to feed, money quickly dried up in their home. In 1974, her mother obtained a visa and came to the US, leaving an older brother in charge of the children. Though her mother sent as much money to the family as she could, there was never enough. Reflecting on the difficulties facing those left behind in Mexico, Graciela said, "While playing in the streets after school at the age of ten, many times I ate from the trash to kill the hunger."

Her mother performed all kinds of menial tasks to earn enough to bring her children to the US. She scrubbed

---

floors, picked strawberries, washed dishes in restaurants, and prayed for God's help. When she was able to phone her children, they cried, saying, "Please come home or take us with you." Though her mother had left to provide for her children, Graciela felt abandoned.

Eventually, her mother was able to bring Graciela to the US and enrolled her in school the day after her arrival.[27] Her mother told her that education was the key to having a good life. At the age of nineteen, Graciela married, but instead of finding happiness, her life turned into a nightmare as her husband became unloving and abusive. Graciela felt she had no reason to live. A sister, however, would tell her, "I am praying for you," which Graciela resented. She told her sister, "You will never make me believe in your Jesus." But as someone once observed, "Human extremity is God's opportunity." Seeing how her sister's life had been transformed by faith in Jesus Christ, Graciela eventually fell to her knees and surrendered, "screaming within for God's help." When she awakened the next morning, her distress had turned to joy, peace, and a tranquility that she could not explain. Her life transformed. She found the strength to leave her abusive marriage.

---

[27] All of the fourteen children not only immigrated to the US but went into medicine as physicians, psychiatrists, nurses, and other related professions.

Shortly thereafter, in 2002, she felt compelled to use her nursing skills and talent for a medical mission in the Congo. She returned smiling, having experienced love as she brought healing to suffering people. Following that trip, she did the same thing in Southern Mexico, then Kenya, then Latin American countries, and then in Ukraine, where she felt a special affinity for the people.

During her work as a nurse in a hospital, Graciela discovered that placing her hands on her patients' hands brought comfort and calmness. Reaching beyond nursing skills, she went back to school for sixteen months and became a certified massage therapist.

Working as a nurse, Graciela took care of a hospice patient who passed away. The patient's husband, Ron Lacey, was impressed with Graciela's care, and in time a friendship developed between them. After sharing her testimony with Ron, a gracious, loving gentleman with a heart for others, the two of them became involved in church outreaches to different parts of the world. In 2005, they married and began serving the Lord together as a married couple.

When Ron retired from a career in aerospace, both he and Graciela decided that God was leading them to Ukraine, where each of them developed a unique ministry. Today, Graciela uses her skills as a massage therapist and teaches others to do the same thing. Ron teaches Celebrate Recovery, a Christ-centered program leading others to recover from hurts, habits, and hang-ups. Both of them are involved in teaching English as a second language.

Graciela says, "It is wonderful how God changed my life. It is through following the teachings of Jesus Christ and knowing that he forgives all our sin that my life became beautiful."

Takeaway Thought

Your hands can be used by God in many ways. Graciela Lacey used hers to serve, comfort, and help bring healing to people. Find ways to be a blessing to someone today. It can even be as simple as giving somebody a pat on the back or a warm hug.

40

MARY,
THE MOTHER OF JESUS

The Woman Who Bore the Son of God

No one ever had a closer relationship with Jesus than did his mother, Mary. If ever there was a woman of destiny, it was her. In the opening verses of the gospel that bears his name, Luke, a medical doctor turned disciple of Jesus, tells the story. An angel is sent by God to Nazareth, a humble, out-of-the way city. The angel appeared to a young woman engaged to be married and said, "Do not be afraid, Mary, for you have found favor with God. And behold, you will conceive in your womb and bear a son, and you shall call his names Jesus." Mary is puzzled: "How will this be, since I am a virgin?" And the angel answered her, "The Holy Spirit will come upon you, and the power of the Most High will overshadow you; therefore the child to be born will be called holy—the Son of God" (Luke 1:30–35 ESV).

Who would believe such a story? Mary did. She responded in faith, saying, "Behold, I am a servant of the Lord. Let it be to me according to your word" (Luke 1:38 ESV). Her fiancé Joseph, however, was dubious. He wanted to quietly break off the engagement until an angel appeared to him in a dream saying, "Joseph, son of David, do not fear to take Mary as your wife, for that which is conceived in her is from the Holy Spirit. She will bear a son, and you shall call his name Jesus, for he will save his people from their sins" (Matthew 1:20–21 ESV). And from that point on, he knew their lives would never be the same.

The next major encounter that Mary and Joseph had with Jesus' identity took place at Passover, when they went to the temple in Jerusalem. After Mary and Joseph started the journey back home, Jesus (now age twelve), unbeknownst to them, stayed in Jerusalem where he astonished the intellectuals of the day, listening to them and asking them difficult questions. Three days later, Jesus connected with his very worried parents. His mother asked, "Son, why have you treated us so?" and Jesus replied, "Did you not know that I must be in my Father's house?" (Luke 2:49). While they did not understand, they realized this son was to impact the world. Luke says, "Jesus grew in wisdom … and in favor with God and man" (Luke 2:52).

After this story, Joseph is not mentioned in the gospels, probably an indication that he had passed away sometime in Jesus' early adulthood, leaving Mary a widow.

At the age of thirty, Jesus began his ministry, calling twelve men to be his closest disciples. No doubt Mary listened to her son as he ministered to hundreds and even thousands, yet she must have felt rejection at times, because Jesus was focused on expanding the family of God and his earthly family was becoming less central. Once when Jesus was teaching, someone told him that his mother and brothers were outside. Jesus replied, "My mother and my brothers are all those who hear God's word and obey it" (Luke 8:21 NLT).

When the tide of public opinion turned and Jesus was crucified, Mary's heart was broken as she witnessed his suffering and pain. On the cross, Jesus turned to John, the youngest of the twelve disciples, and said, "Behold, your mother!" thereby putting his mother in the care of John—who, no doubt, treated her as his own mother in her final years (John 19:27 ESV).

Why is Mary important to the scope of redemption? She was the only person who was present at the birth of Christ and also at his death. Mary knew her Old Testament and the prophecies regarding the coming Messiah. Her Magnificat is a beautiful and poetic hymn of praise and worship (Luke 1:46–55). (Some have pointed out that it is very similar to Hannah's prayer found in 1 Samuel 2:1–10.) Mary shines as an illustration of the fact that God uses humble, dedicated women who are faithful to the Lord and become channels of God's grace and goodness. As Edith Deen wrote of Mary in her book *All the Women of the Bible*, "Though she never traveled any farther than from Palestine to Egypt, and then by donkey, her story still travels to the farthest corners of the earth!"[28]

May God give us many, many more brave women who can follow in Mary's footsteps, making a difference in our world, women of destiny touching the suffering, the lonely, the neglected, and the hurting.

Takeaway Thought

Do you have a heart like Mary's? What will it take for you to say yes to God when he invites you to join him in his great plan of redemption? If you haven't yet, commit yourself to live for the Lord and be willing to do whatever he has called you to do. God can use anybody to change the world. And he can definitely use you.

MORE ABOUT HER STORY

Luke 1:26–56; 2:1–52
Matthew 2:1–23
John 19:25–27

---

[28] Kristine Brown, "3 Things You Didn't Know about Mary (Mother of Jesus) in the Bible," August 27, 2019, *Crosswalk.com*.

Discovering the Path for Your Life

If you sat down across the table from me and asked, "Where do I go from here?" I would suggest you consider the following thoughts gleaned from my own experience working with people for more than sixty years.

1. Be the person God made you to be.

You have been uniquely gifted for what God wants to accomplish in your life. When Paul wrote to the Ephesians and told them to be filled with the Holy Spirit, he prefaced his advice by saying, "Don't be ignorant, but understand the Lord's will [for your life]" (Ephesians 5:17 CEB). The word translated as *ignorant* means "void of understanding" or "without the knowledge of something."

God is far more interested in showing you his will for your life than you are in knowing what it is. George Müeller, a man of great faith, once said, "The steps of a good man are ordered by the Lord, and so are the stops!" This includes you as well. Hold on to your uniqueness—the result of God's design which he will use in his way, in his time, in the place of his choosing.

2. God's enabling accompanies God's calling.

When I wrote my book *Heroes*, I discovered that many of the individuals (both men and women) who have done the greatest exploits for God were seemingly least qualified to accomplish much in life. Those with great talents and education tend to trust their own resources, connections, and abilities, but those who lack much also trust much! As you reflect on the selections in this book, you will see that many—such as Gladys Aylward, who was asked to leave the school she thought would prepare her for ministry—accomplished far more in life than many with better education and talents.

3. Your extremity is God's opportunity.

Was there ever a situation more desperate than that which faced Darlene Deibler Rose in a Japanese concentration camp in World War II, or that which faced Virginia Prodan as she looked down the barrel of an assassin's gun? Nothing is impossible with God, and I am fully persuaded it is better to know God's power and grace in the hour of need than to never know or experience his care and providence. When you are at your extremity—your most challenging moment—that is God's opportunity to accomplish the impossible.

4. "God's work done in God's way will never lack God's supply."

 So said Hudson Taylor, the missionary to China and founder of the China Inland Mission. With that conviction, I began broadcasting in 1963 with the assurance that God had called us and would provide for our needs—and should he not do that, we would call it quits, and I would go into business and support others. Years ago, we learned that God, who knows what our needs are, will provide in his way, and in so doing, we knew it was him and not clever promotion or manipulation that connected his vast resources with our needs.

5. The gifts and the calling of God are irrevocable.

The apostle Paul wrote to the Corinthians, saying, "For God's gifts and his call are irrevocable" (Romans 11:29). There are many different seasons to life, and a wise person recognizes that God may redirect your life to a different location or another kind of ministry or work. Amy Carmichael first went to Japan, then China, then Ceylon, then back to Britain for a period of time before she finally traveled to India where she ministered for the rest of her life. She knew that she had been called, and the Holy Spirit guided her to the place of his choosing, not necessarily hers. Following Jim Elliot's death, his wife Elisabeth made contact with the group who had taken his life and lived among them translating Scripture, but eventually returned to the US where she impacted thousands of lives through her books and through teaching and speaking engagements.

6. The longest journey in the world begins with the first step.

With Gladys Aylward, the first step towards getting to China was to open a savings account where she deposited a small pittance every payday. If you feel that God is calling you to serve him, taking the good news of God's love and forgiveness to those who are living in darkness, realize that adequate preparation equips you to better accomplish what God wants you to do. Talk with your pastor or an older, mature Christian whom you respect, and their counsel as well as prayers and perhaps, eventually, the availability of financial support will encourage you and confirm your calling.

7. Follow your passion.

There is an intertwining of your natural aptitudes and your spiritual gifts. Some, such as Shelia Leech, can handle trekking into a jungle to provide medical care, sleeping with a mosquito net over her, coping with the presence of snakes that wanted to share a sleeping bag. Others might be unable to live in the jungle but can serve in an office or at a mission's headquarters, or provide support as a missionary pilot.

What's your passion in life? Do you enjoy teaching? Then perhaps that is your calling. Are children very special to you? Then remember that Lillian Trasher's orphanage, which had as many as two hundred children in it, was begun when she visited a dying woman and the woman's last words were to ask Lillian to take her baby lest the grandmother throw the infant into the Nile River. I would encourage you to ask, "Is what I enjoy doing running parallel with what God is, indeed, calling me to do?" If so, better get moving! You will never be happier and find more joy than when you are serving the King of Kings, driving back the darkness, and making a difference in our world, one person at a time.

For you, dear reader, God's very best is yet ahead!

Harold J. Sala

I would like to hear your thoughts. You can reach me at info@guidelines.org.

Other Books You May Enjoy

Journey Into Grace by Darlene Sala, Bonnie Sala, and Luisa Collopy

More Precious Than Diamonds by Darlene Sala

Age Is Just A Number by Harold and Darlene Sala

Available at www.guidelines.org

About Dr. Harold Sala
and the Ministry of Guidelines

D r. Harold Sala founded Guidelines International Ministries in 1963 and pioneered the five-minute daily devotional on Christian radio. Dr. Sala's program, *Guidelines for Living,* continues to transform lives with its practical, biblical message. Now available in over 20 translations, *Guidelines for Living* is heard in Central Asia, Asia, Latin America, the Middle East and Africa, encouraging new believers, reaching the unreached and ministering to the persecuted.

Guidelines International Ministries was awarded the 2014 Milestone Award by National Religious Broadcasters, celebrating Guidelines' nearly six-decade commitment to proclaiming the gospel and *Guidelines for Living* received the 2019 Radio Impact Award.

In addition to Dr. Sala's legacy of nearly 14,000 audio and video devotionals, he has authored over 60 books published in 19 languages. Some of his works have been released and distributed by Barbour, B&H Publishers, Christian Publications, Inc., Harvest House, Moody Press, Rose Publishing, Thomas Nelson, and OMF Literature, Inc.

Dr. Sala, who holds a PhD in English Bible from Bob Jones University, is a well-loved international speaker and Bible teacher. Married to Darlene for over 60 years, the Salas live close to their adult children and their families in Southern California.

Also from Harold Sala

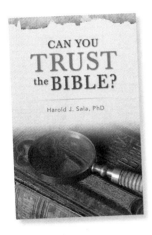

CAN YOU TRUST the **BIBLE?**

Skeptics, seekers, and Christians alike may wonder:

- How did we get the Bible in its current form?
- What does it mean when we say the Bible is inspired?
- How do we know that the Bible has been accurately preserved?
- Is science at odds with the Bible?

Dr. Harold Sala presents compelling reasons why you can believe the most trustworthy book of all time.

Evidence presented includes:

- The powerful testimony of manuscript evidence
- How archaeology supports biblical accuracy
- What fulfilled prophecies prove
- Ways faith and science are compatible
- Firsthand experiences that confirm the authenticity of the Bible

Discover the reasons why you can trust the Bible, and then decide what the Bible will mean to you personally. Ignore it, trivialize it, deny it, or embrace it: Let your heart—and your mind—decide.

Can You Trust the Bible? ISBN 9781628629644

Available at www.hendricksonrose.com